A2Z+

El Lissitzky, *Sportsmen*, USSR, c.1920

A2Z+

ALPHABETS
&
SIGNS

Edited by Julian Rothenstein

Texts by MEL GOODING

PRINCETON ARCHITECTURAL PRESS · NEW YORK

Published by
Princeton Architectural Press
A McEvoy Group company
202 Warren Street
Hudson, NY 12534
www.papress.com

Published in arrangement with Redstone Press
7a St Lawrence Terrace
London, UK W10 5SU
www.theredstoneshop.com

Manufactured by 1010 Printing International Limited, China
21 20 19 18 4 3 2 1

ISBN: 978-1-61689-707-9

Design: Julian Rothenstein
Copyeditor: Nolan Boomer
Artwork: Otis Marchbank
Production: Geoff Barlow

For Princeton Architectural Press:
Project Editors: Rob Shaeffer and Nolan Boomer
Cover design: Paul Wagner, based on a design by Azi Rad

Thanks to: Ariadne Arendt, David Batterham, Lutz Becker, Pavel Büchler,
Pablo Butcher, Rhiannon Gooding, Richard Hollis, Nasreen Kabir,
Hiang Kee, Sasha Lurye, Rick Poynor, Simon Rendall, Erika Rothenberg,
Bertram Schmidt-Friderichs, Mimi Thompson, Brian Webb

Special thanks to: Ryan Alcazar, Janet Behning, Nicola Brower,
Abby Bussel, Benjamin English, Jan Cigliano Hartman, Kristen Hewitt,
Lia Hunt, Valerie Kamen, Jennifer Lippert, Sara McKay, Eliana Miller,
Nina Pick, Sara Stemen, Marisa Tesoro, and Joseph Weston of
Princeton Architectural Press —Kevin C. Lippert, publisher

Library of Congress Cataloging-in-Publication Data

Names: Rothenstein, Julian, 1948- editor. | Gooding, Mel, writer of added text.
Title: A2Z+ : alphabets & signs / edited by Julian Rothenstein ; texts by Mel Gooding.
Other titles: ABZ
Description: New York : Princeton Architectural Press, 2018.
Identifiers: LCCN 2017048894 | ISBN 9781616897079 (paperback)
Subjects: LCSH: Alphabets. | Lettering. | Signs and signboards. | BISAC:
  DESIGN / Graphic Arts / Typography. | DESIGN / History & Criticism.
  DESIGN / Graphic Arts / General.
Classification: LCC NK3600 .A28 2018 | DDC 659.13/42--dc23
LC record available at https://lccn.loc.gov/2017048894

A Man of Letters, UK, c.1890

CONTENTS

MEL GOODING:

INTRODUCING *A2Z+*

"Give me twenty-six soldiers of lead and I will conquer the world." Benjamin Franklin (attributed)

I: Alphabets and Other Signs

Of the making of alphabets there is no end. This book has been made to illustrate that fact, and celebrate it. As an abstract written sign, the letter developed from the pictogram, the simple drawing that accompanied speech into the making of the first human culture. The sign must exist—drawn by a finger in sand, marked in ash or ochre on the cave wall, scratched into clay by a stick—before the sound can be attached to it. All letters begin as signs, writes Victor Hugo, and all signs begin as images. In a famous and not entirely fanciful little essay, the great novelist finds in the modern alphabet everything from the image of the simplest shelter, to the portent of human destiny and the sign of God:

A is the roof, the gable with its crossbeam, the arch; or it is two friends greeting, who embrace and shake hands; D is the human back; B is the D on the D, back on the back, the hump; C is the crescent, the moon; E is the foundations, the pillar, the console and the architrave, all architecture in a single letter; F is the gibbet; G is the French horn; H is a facade with two towers; I is the war machine launching its projectile; J is the ploughshare and the horn of plenty; K is the angle of reflection equal to the angle of incidence, a key to geometry; L is the leg and foot; M is a mountain or a camp with tents pitched in pairs; N is a gate with a diagonal bar; O is the sun; P is a porter with a load on his back; Q is a rump with a tail; R is the porter resting on his staff; S is a serpent; T is a hammer; U is the urn, V the vase, which are easily confused; Y is a tree, the fork of two roads, the confluence of two rivers, the head of a donkey or an ox, a stemmed glass, a lily on its stalk, a man praying with arms up-stretched; X is crossed swords, a battle: who will win we do not know, so the mystics made it the sign of destiny and the algebraists the sign of the unknown; Z is lightning, the sign of God: ... that is what the alphabet contains.

As the ancient Celtic proverb has it, every force evolves a form: in human affairs necessity creates energies, and out of energies evolve technologies. Of course, no sooner had alphabets come into existence, together with all the endless possibilities of variations in letterforms and calligraphic style, than they were joined by infinite varieties of sign, symbol, and image, illuminating, elaborating and reinforcing the verbal message. Much later, out of the big bang of early Renaissance printing technology, there was an ever-expanding new universe, the Gutenberg galaxy of visual-linguistic constellations. *A2Z+* (a title which combines letter and sign, beginning and end) presents a dazzling sampling of this cosmos in its (mostly) modern manifestations.

With the advent of printing—the defining technology of the modern world, the *sine qua non* of other modern technologies, perhaps the single most important invention since drawing—came the need for different letterforms to serve a multitude of diverse functions. Every job demands the lettering that will serve its purposes best. The stonemason's lapidary, the stencil-maker's schematic, the needleworker's stitchable, the signwriters' eye-catching typeface, as well as the manifold forms that are necessary to the printer's trade proper: so many alphabets for so many tasks in so many media! Each has a character and a face of its own, each bears the imprint of its time and the marks of its milieu. Alphabets come in unending diversity: in some the letterforms are pure and simple, in others, complex, complicated, extravagant, or fantastic. There are modest alphabets and flamboyant alphabets, silly alphabets and sad ones. Alphabets proliferate. In literate societies they are an index of human diversity: children that learn to write invent their own, as distinctive as their fingerprints. Every alphabet presents an orchestration of the letters to the eye, a systematic optical abstract, a visual matrix out of which any number of possible messages might be composed.

II: The Revival of Classical Typography

Not all alphabets are equal. Some are elegant, reflecting the grace and intelligence of their makers and users, fit for the transparent setting of subtle and beautiful language; some are workaday and simple, democratic in spirit, apt for plain writing, plain printing; others are squat and blocky, their ugly faces betraying the brutality of their time and place in history; others are ludic, capricious, or idiosyncratic, drawing attention to their formal waywardness. As functional visual systems designed for communicative purposes, printed alphabets speak of their time and place, and assume recognizable styles. They invite contemplation as freestanding artifacts of their cultures, variously perfect, flawed, or simply queer. In every case they are aesthetically expressive and culturally shaped.

It is no contradiction that for many typographers, printers, and publishers, especially those concerned with the setting of prose in books and newspapers, the perfect typeface is one in which the alphabet becomes invisible (so to speak) as the reader apprehends the matter carried by the complicated and rigorous arrangements of its individual characters. These perfectionists imagine the typeset page as a clear window upon meaning; every letterform is balanced, and every relation between letters in words, or words in sentences, is designed to minimize distraction between the message and the medium. "Printing should be invisible," writes Beatrice Warde, the writer and publicist for the Monotype Corporation in its golden years. (Monotype, founded in 1896, was the major supplier of typefaces in both the United States and the United Kingdom for much of the early twentieth century.) For the redoubtable Stanley Morison, the doyen of typographers in that period, there was no room for argument: typography was the efficient means to an essentially utilitarian and only accidentally aesthetic end. "Therefore, any disposition of printing material which, whatever the intention, has the effect of coming between author and reader is wrong."

For British typographers like Morison and Eric Gill, as well as the American Bruce Rogers and the Dutchman Jan van Krimpen, revivalists of the great classic typefaces as well as inventors of elegant new functional ones, the letter must modestly and discreetly serve the text: "If readers do not notice the consummate reticence and rare discipline of a new type, it is probably a good letter," writes Morison. *Clarity* and *legibility* were the watchwords of these militant traditionalists, and in the UK and the US these words carried their histories into the great typographical revival of the years between the world wars.

Centaur

Aa Qq Rr

Aa Qq Rr

abcdefghijklm
nopqrstuvwxyz
0123456789

Centaur designed by Bruce Rogers

Didot

Aa Qq Rr

Aa Qq Rr

abcdefghijklm
nopqrstuvwxyz
0123456789

Didot produced by the Didot family

American Type Founders Specimen Book and Catalogue (New Jersey, 1923)

The task of the type-designer, as they conceived it, was to achieve a balanced face in which each letter would aspire to tonal equality with every other, and to a non-assertive unity of effect. The printer's job was to set the page with a symmetrical balance, vertically centering the text in such a way as to afford the least visual disturbance possible, and to ornament with taste and discretion only where the text allowed and the accepted aesthetic of the page would be positively served. There was an ethical purpose to this aesthetic: clarity of delivery enhanced communication; knowledge and argument conveyed with economy was essential to democratic understanding and thus to individual and collective freedom of thought.

These rigorous ideals, based on principles of public service in a spirit disposed to the democratic dissemination of knowledge and ideas, were advocated with a stolid eloquence in the writings of Morison, Gill, Rogers, and others. They were exemplified with grace in beautifully produced publications such as, in England, Francis Meynell's *Typography* (1923), Morison's type journal *The Fleuron* (seven issues from 1923 to 1932) and Oliver Simon's magazine *Signature* (first issue November 1935). In the States, Rogers directed the typography of many beautiful books for Riverside Press (Cambridge, Massachusetts), for Harvard University Press, and for the Metropolitan Museum of Art, where he designed Maurice de Guérin's *The Centaur*, for which he created the celebrated eponymous typeface, itself based on the beautiful typography of the fifteenth-century Frenchman Nicolas Jenson, based in Venice. Reflecting the taste and discipline of this classical movement, there were published on both sides of the Atlantic through the '20s and '30s a remarkable succession of superb printers' type-specimen books: notable among many others in the UK were those issued by the Curwen Press in 1928, Richard Clay & Sons in 1930, the Kynoch Press in 1934, and W. S. Cowell in 1947; and in the US the magnificent, wide-ranging and encyclopedic *American Type Founders Specimen Book and Catalogue* (New Jersey, 1923).

These latter publications contained complete alphabets set in every face used by the printer—in uppercase, lowercase, bold, and italic—and in their various sizes, and frequently carried demonstration pages of text set and beautifully illustrated with original lithography. Splendid as they might be, these specimen books were in essence intentionally commercial, and they were limited, of course, to those type alphabets the printers actually stocked and used in books, magazines, cards, posters, handbills, etc. It was nevertheless understood, from the earliest days of commercial printing, that the jobbing printer was necessarily at the heart of democratic communications, the essential journeyman (the daily worker!) in the cause of social change and reform, and printers were notable for their radical politics. In the *American Type Founders Manual of 1941*, some of the specimen pages were set with direct and eloquent statements of the democratic principles and functions of printing: "Giving voice to the countless thousands who tell their story in the printed word is the function of type." Other manuals on both sides of the Atlantic often contained witty, cryptic political messages. It should not be a surprise that one of the best manuals containing directions and advice on the styling of publications of the postwar days of hope was Michael Middleton's *Soldiers of Lead*, issued by the British Labour Party in 1948, with an epigraph from *Areopagitica*, Milton's classic polemic against censorship of the printed word.

III: The Modernist Revolution in Typography

While the revivalists, high-minded and idealistic, but fundamentally conservative, were determining the new directions of book, magazine, and newspaper design in the UK and the US, elsewhere, in Continental Europe, things were radically different. In Russia, Germany, and the Netherlands, an altogether new kind of revolution in typography was taking place, inspired by the utopian ideals of modernism, and led not only by letter designers and typographers, but also by major artists. In the philosophy of De Stijl and Kurt Schwitters's Merz, in the publications of the Bauhaus, in the work of El Lissitzky, László Moholy-Nagy, Herbert Bayer, H. N. Werkman, Jan Tschichold, and many others, a new and aggressively asymmetrical typography was adopted and advocated for universal use in the new age. To the sans-serif types of Tschichold's *Die neue Typographie* were accorded the attributes of an honest and unornamented beauty and clarity appropriate to the rational life of modern humankind.

What is more, the letter, freed from subordination to the word, leapt into visibility and proclaimed itself a concrete and independent component of the printed message. The setting of the message itself—poem or prose, information, advertisement, or propaganda—aspired to the condition of the graphic abstract image, dynamically entering the eye and the mind, challenging critical response, and inviting reaction and reflection on its own account. Asymmetrical and emphasizing the diagonal, a new style of photography was enlisted into the cause of communicative urgency, exemplified in different ways and in different moods in the work of such innovators as Alexander Rodchenko and André Kertész. Letter itself became sign: the page, the poster, the book jacket became art forms in their own right; the word joined in the modern visual dance.

This collaboration with modernist art was based upon deep affinities. Behind these exciting developments in typography were the pioneering modernist abstractions of Kazimir Malevich, Piet Mondrian, František Kupka, and Theo van Doesburg. "There is a connection between modern typography and modern architecture," wrote Jan Tschichold in his classic exposition *Asymmetrical Typography* (1935), "but the new typography does not derive from the new architecture; rather both derive from the new painting, which has given to both a new significance of form. … [An abstract painting] is an instrument of spiritual power, a conception of harmony. It is an appeal to order, a means to the improvement of mankind. It is not passive but dynamic." The printed page was just such an instrument, its energetic aesthetic having political and ethical purpose.

In France the stylish and chic dispositions of letter and motif of the more advanced journals and magazines of the modern period derived, typically, from homegrown artistic sources. They were appropriated with Gallic insouciance from: the graphic wit and vigor of Toulouse-Lautrec, the jazzy *moderne* of Art Deco, the diverse variations of *mise-en-page*, the play of illustration against text in the great *livres d'artistes*, and the typographical-poetic experiments of Mallarmé and Apollinaire. In the present volume this elegant, eclectic stylism is especially celebrated in the pages from the Paris journal of printing design *Arts et Métiers Graphiques*.

IV: The Pleasures of the Page

The letter is the point at which the structures of language meet the ground of the visible. It arrives in human culture long after speech in the order of things, long after the sounds uttered by humankind at its beginning had separated into words and been organized into grammatical systems of meaning. It was preceded in the world by visual signs, and has forever since been constantly accompanied by them. The visual sign, in its simple directness, is the means by which the sounds of speech found their way toward the letter and the written word. In a book such as this, which presents alphabets, signs, and images in many forms and many styles, and which is intended not only for use or inspiration by designers, artists, poets, and writers, but also for the visual and intellectual pleasure of anyone who loves letters in their infinite variety, it is proper for the sign and the image to be a vigorous and enlivening presence to the letter.

We live in an age in which the ease of recourse to diverse alphabets and letters is unprecedented, and in which more alphabets have been invented than ever before in history. In the period of modernism, to whose progressive and humane principles we pay homage in this book, there was access as never before to good design and visual diversity. In newspapers, magazines, and books, on book jackets and film posters, in the packaging of objects and the advertisement of goods and services, on buildings, hoardings, in streets and public buildings, in the subway, on the railway, and on the buses, wherever information was conveyed, there was evidence of the most intelligent and aesthetically sophisticated combination of utility, wit, and beauty. We may feel that some of the economy and visual clarity of this graphic landscape of letter and sign has been lost to postmodern clutter and confusion.

This book reproduces a series of signwriters' alphabets intended to find their public realization on shop fronts and bar signs, elegant eye charts for the optician's patient, letters and signs for technical manuals, fine typographies for beautiful books, a magisterial Constructivist alphabetic ballet, and so on. Every task demands its own kind of alphabet; every new purpose evolves an appropriate new lettering. This book is not like the many alphabet books and surveys (utilitarian collections of particular alphabets) that already exist; nor is it a type-specimen book or a manual of style and layout. It has no program and it has no system of presentation; it confuses categories and obeys no rules. It reflects, rather, the taste and interests of the editor: his affection for the wayward as well as the rigorous in matters of design and typography, his love for all manner of alphabets, lettering, typography, and sign-making. It delights also in the multifarious signs and images that jostle the printed word and create the variegated visual world of the page—photographs and montages, drawings, patterns, printers' fleurons and flourishes, decorations and clichés, vignettes, trademarks, and logos. It is a book made for all lovers of letters and signs, for their use perhaps, and certainly for their delight.

Mel Gooding
July 2017

Note: This introduction is adapted and expanded from the introductory texts to *Alphabets and Other Signs* and *ABZ: More Alphabets and other Signs* (Redstone Press, London 1991 and 2004, respectively).

Chinese-style alphabet, UK, c.1940

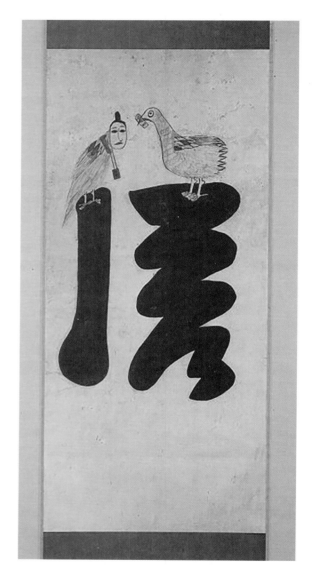

Folk calligraphy, Japan, early 19th century

Folk calligraphy: character for prosperity, China, c.1880

Magazine cover, *Modern Sketch* (No. 19), China, 1930s

ab

b bcddef ghChrijkkl m n appgdrss tuvwwxgyz

Indian-style alphabet, UK, c.1940

3039   3040   3041   3042

3048   3047   3012   3051   3052

3053   3054   3055   3056

3057   3058   3059   3032   3033

3063   3064   3065   3066   3067   3068

THE MADRAS TYPE FOUNDRY, - - MADRAS-

From a typefounders' catalogue, India, c.1955

Cinema poster, India, 1970s. Courtesy N. M. Kabir/Hyphen Films Ltd. collection

Sheffield
1-5 A.M. 21st November 1900.

Agnes Tonisa Johnston Yule
is born in Sheffield on the 21st November
1900 at 1-5 A.M. when the level of Leo was
24° 38' on the 29th lunar day when Moon
occupied the Sign Libra under the Sixteenth
asterism Bisakha.

May God grant her long life and prosperity.

First page of horoscope album (handmade, with thirteen further astrological charts), India, 1900

Playing cards for children published by Chitrashala Press, India, c.1940

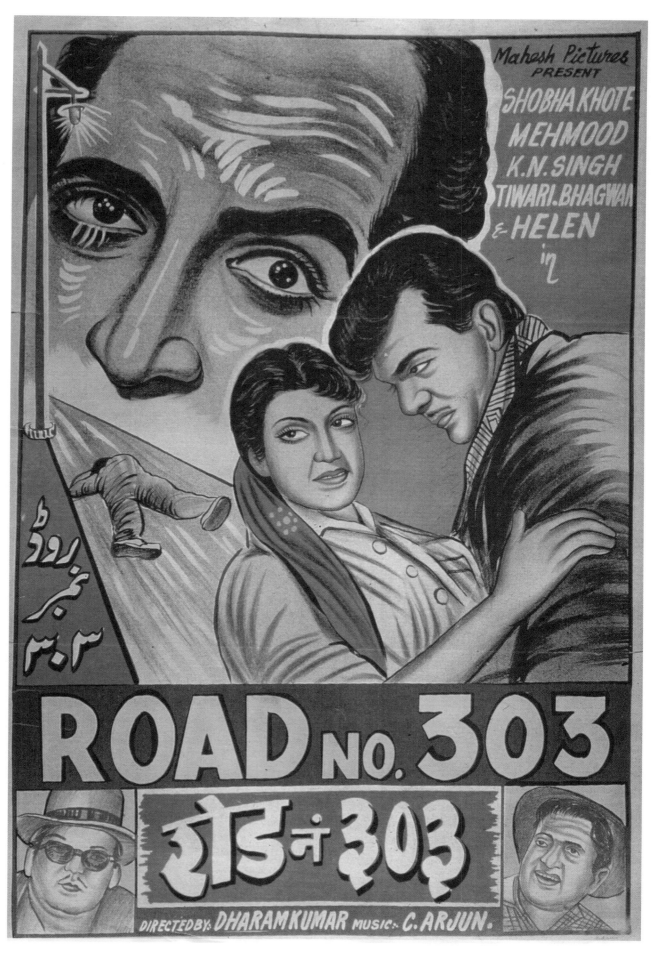

Poster, *Road No. 303*, India, c.1954. Courtesy N. M. Kabir/Hyphen Films Ltd. collection

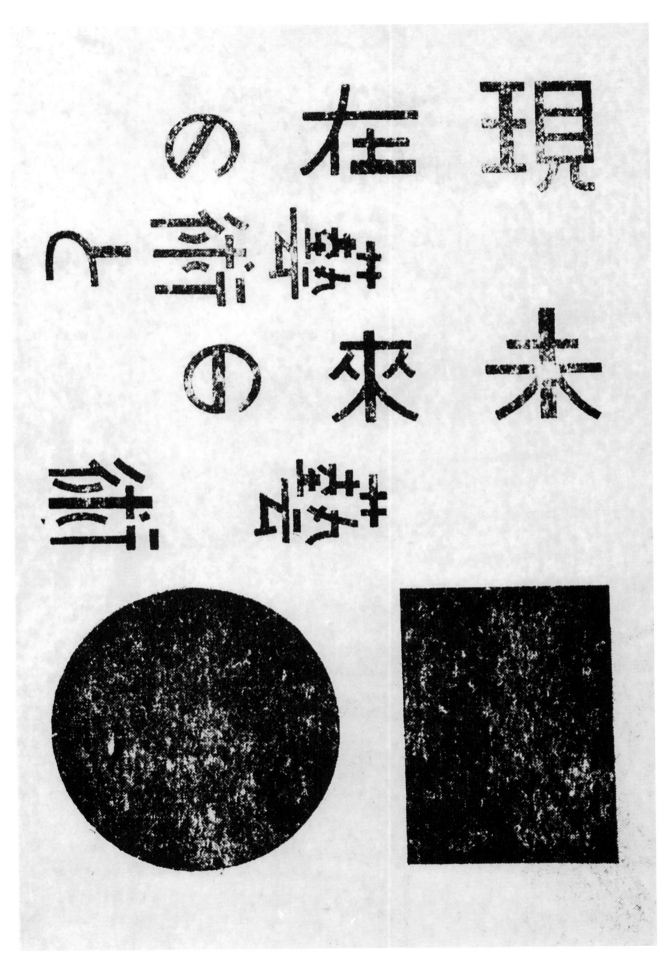

Book cover, Japan, date unknown

Book cover, *The Sea Was Blue behind the Mountain*, illustrated by Shinta Naga, Japan, 1930s

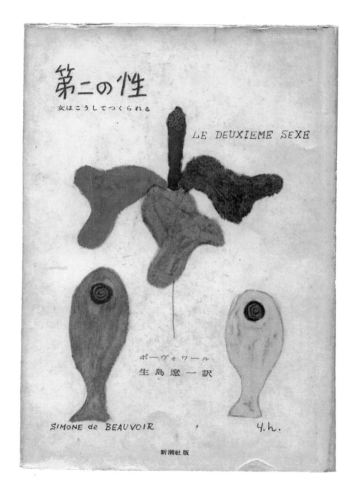

Book cover, *The Second Sex* by Simone de Beauvoir, designed by Yasuji Hanamori, Japan, 1950s

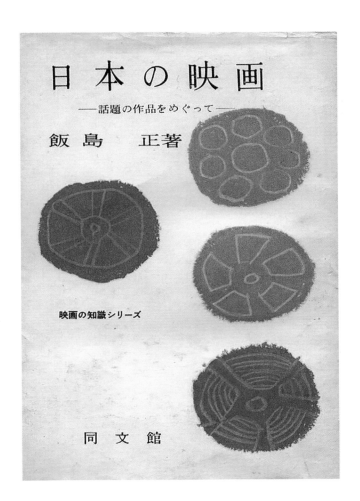

Book cover, *Japanese Films* by Tadashi Iijima, Japan, 1930s

Magazine cover, *The Bungei Shunju* (a literary journal), Japan, 1946

Book cover designed by Yasuji Hanamori, Japan, 1970s

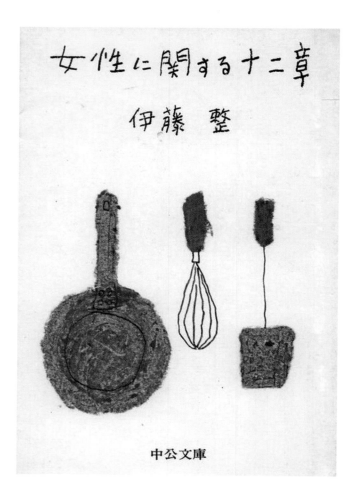

Book cover designed by Yasuji Hanamori, Japan, 1954

Book cover designed by Yasuji Hanamori, Japan, 1946

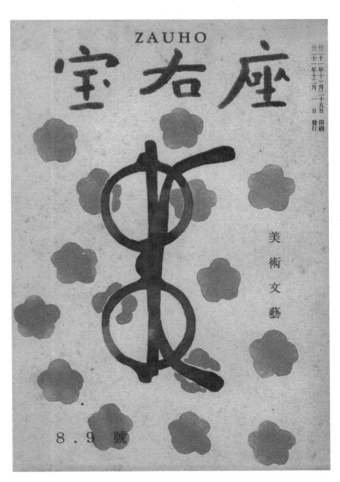

Magazine cover, *Zauho* (a journal of art and literature), Japan, c.1941

Magazine cover, *Mavo* (No.3), Japan, 1924

Japanese-style alphabet, source and date unknown

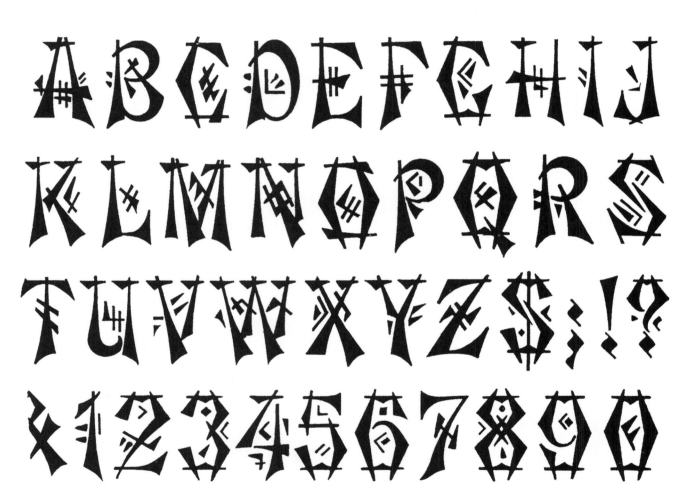

Japanese-style lettering, USA, c.1970

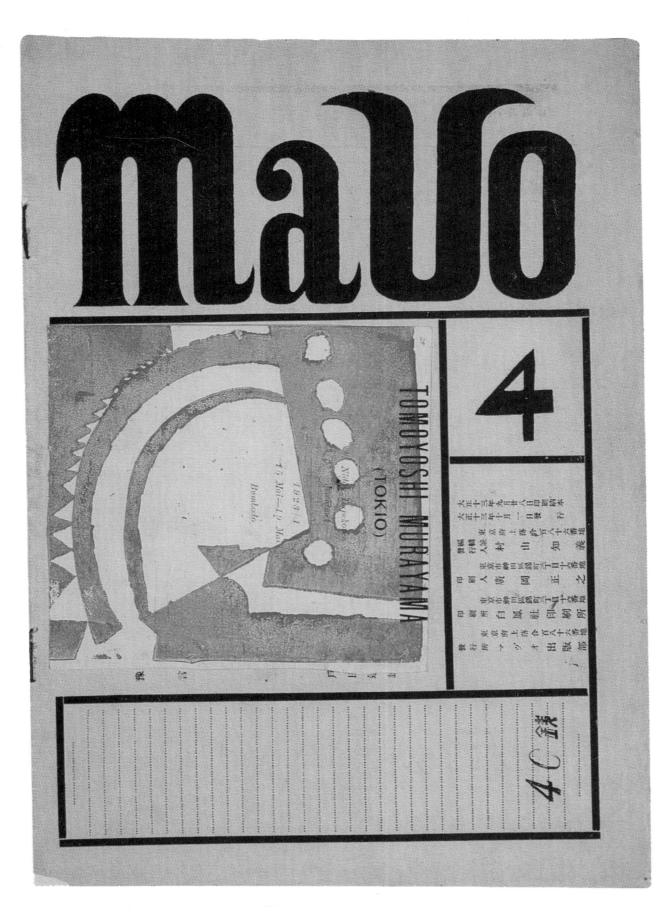

Magazine cover, *Mavo* (No.4), with a linocut by Toda Tatsuo, Japan, 1924

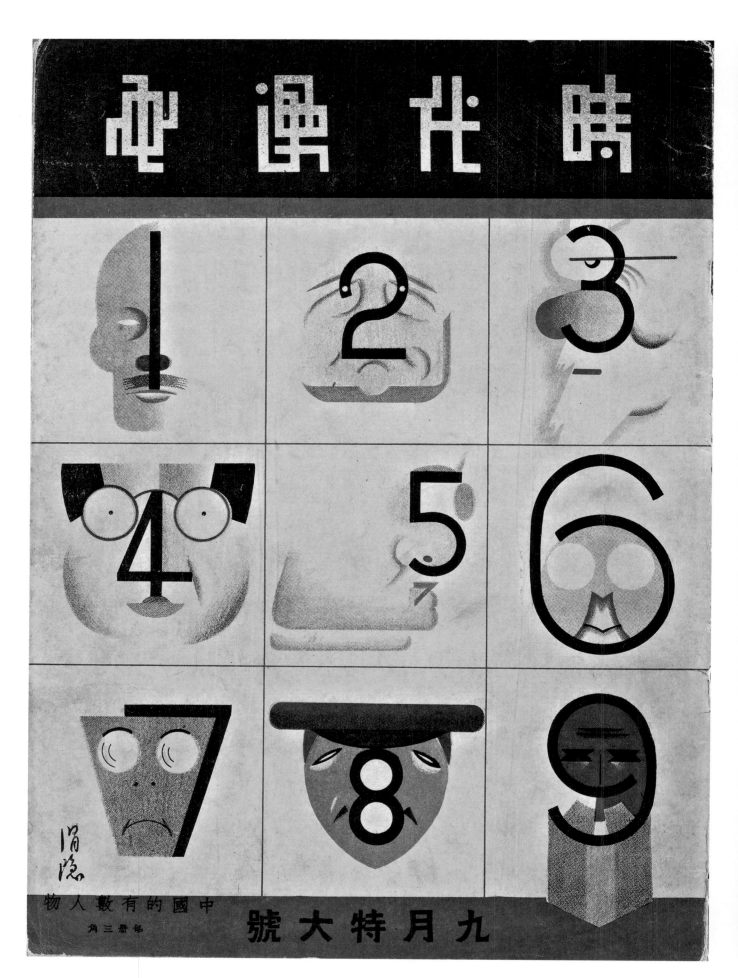

Magazine cover, *Modern Sketch* (No.9). reads "Caricatures: Who Counts in China?", illustrated by Chen Juanyin, China, 1930s

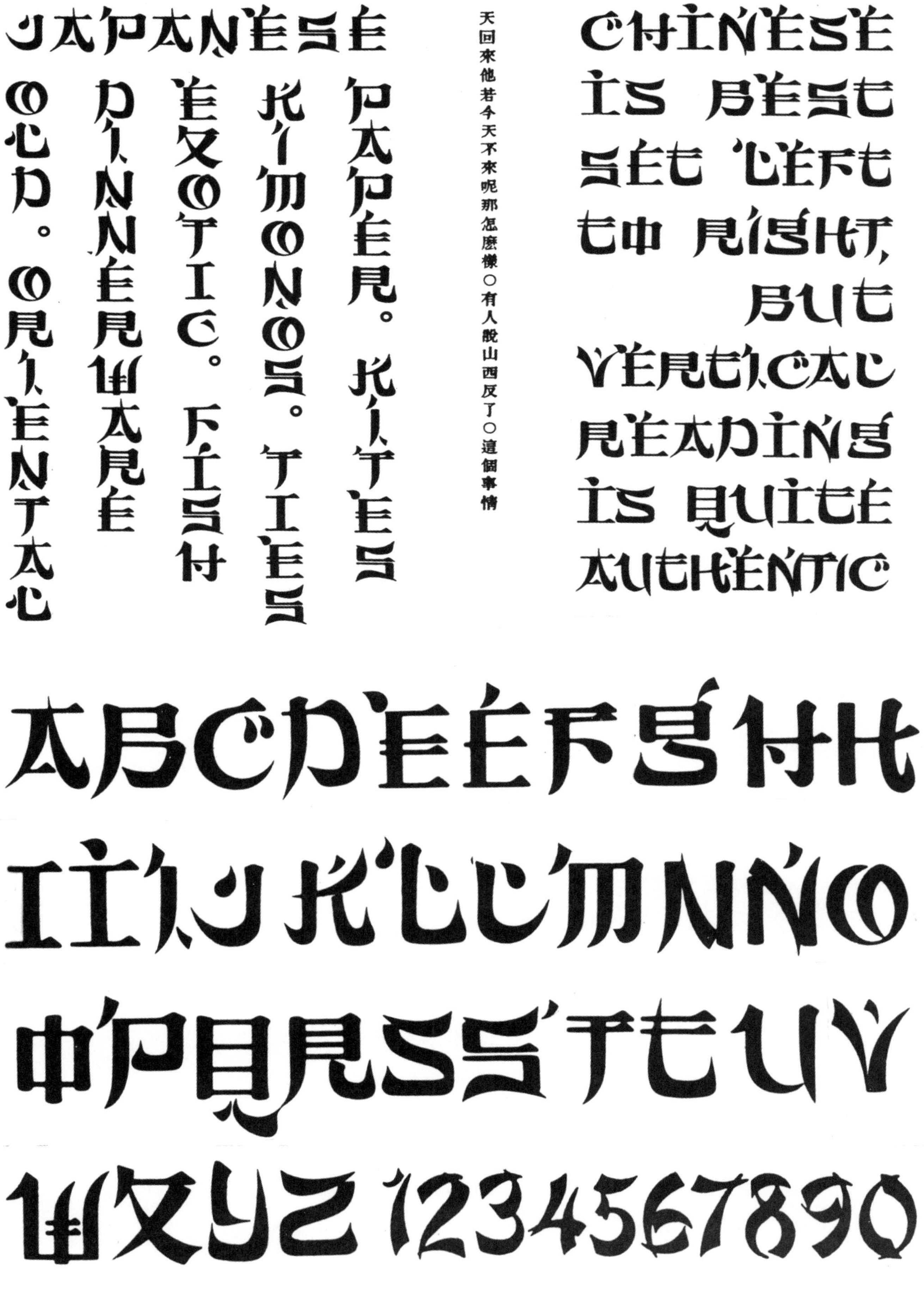

JAPANESE

PAPER. KITES. KIMONOS. EXOTIC. FISH. TIES. DINNERWARE. OLD. ORIENTAL

天回來他若今天不來呢那怎麼樣〇有人說山西反了〇這個事情

CHINESE
IS BEST SEE LEFT TO RIGHT, BUT VERTICAL READING IS QUITE AUTHENTIC

ABCDEFGHI
IJKLMNO
中PQRSSTUV
WXYZ1234567890

Chinese- and Japanese-style alphabets

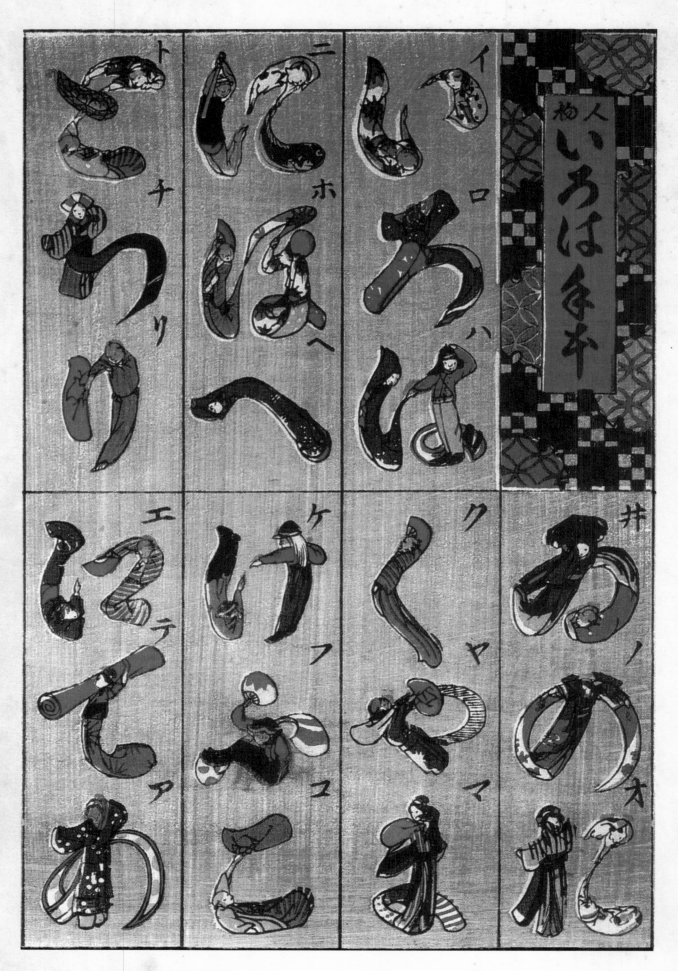

Classroom poster, *47 Characters for Easy Learning* (detail), Japan, 1864

Erika Rothenberg, *America's Joyous Future*, USA, 1990. © Erika Rothenberg

From *The Marsh Stencil Machine Co.* catalogue, USA, c.1947, Courtesy Eric Finkel collection

Model S ¾″ Machine cuts this size stencil, one to four lines, any length. For marking medium sized shipments. Size of Machine 21″ x 16″ x 10″ high. Weight 100 lbs. Packed 145 lbs.

Size of Stencil Board for Model S ¾″ Machine

1-line 3″ x 20″   3-line 5″ x 20″
2-line 4″ x 20″   4-line 6″ x 20″

This is an actual reproduction of the stencil characters cut by Model S (¾″ size) Marsh Stencil Machine.

| ¾″ |

ABCDEFGHIJ
KLMNOPQRST
UVWXYZ' /&,
2345 6789-.

This is an actual reproduction of the stencil characters cut by the Model R (1″ size) **Marsh Stencil Machine.**

Model R 1″ Machine cuts this size, one to four lines, any length. For marking large shipments. Size of machine 24″ x 18″ x 10″ high. Weight 145 lbs. Packed 195 lbs.

Size of Stencil Board for Model R 1″ Machine.

1-line 4″ x 20″ or 24″   3-line 6″ x 20″ or 24″
2-line 5″ x 20″ or 24″   4-line 7″ x 20″ or 24″

| 1″ |

ABCDEFGHIJ
KLMNOPQRST
UVWXYZ' /&,
2345 6789-.

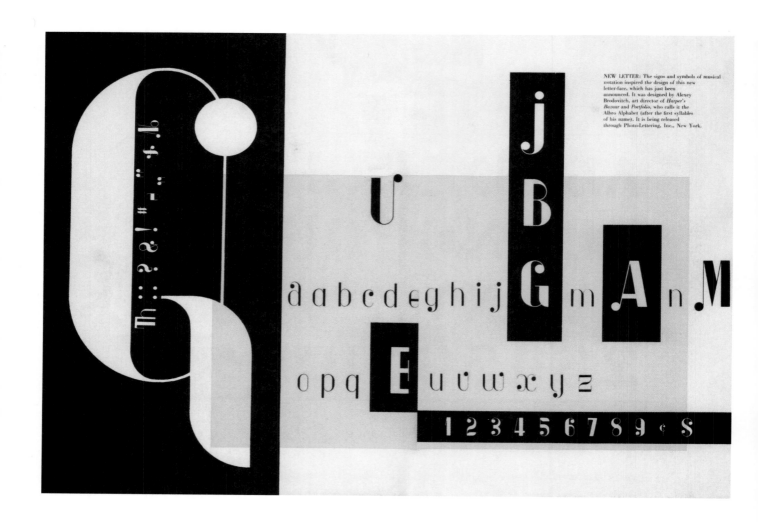

ABCDEFGHIJKLMNOPQRSTUVWXYZ

abcdefghijklmnopqrstuvwxyz

0123456789 [{@¡!#$%&::'"}]

Typeface design by Alexey Brodovitch, from *Portfolio* (No. 1), USA, 1950

VWMNK
OCSQGA
XYZIEFL
UDBRP
JTH ;,!?:

Alphabet design from *Lettering Art in Modern Use* by William Dressler, USA, 1952

RKO

MEETS THE CHALLENGE OF 1951...

R K O RADIO PICTURES

with top product for every showdate of the year...January through December...

AND HERE IT IS!...

Promotional leaflet for RKO Radio Pictures, USA, 1951. Courtesy N. M. Kabir/Hyphen Films Ltd. collection

A B C D E F G H I J K L M N O P Q R
S T U V W X Y Z ★ 1 2 3 4 5 6 7 8 9 ★ ?

a b c d e f g h i j k l m
n o p q r s t u v w x y z

VARIETY
·
VARIETY

– it's the RESULT that COUNTS !

44

A B C D E F G H I J K L
M N O P Q R S T U V W X
Y Z 1 2 3 4 5 6 7 8 9 ?

VARIETY

A B C D E F G H I J K L
M N O P Q R S T U V W
X Y Z 1 2 3 4 5 6 7 8 9

VARIETY

American moderne: typefaces designed by Paul Carlyle and Guy Oring, from *Letters and Lettering*, USA, 1938. Courtesy Brian Webb collection

abcdefghikl moprstuvw xyz

From a typefounders' manual, USA, c.1950

James Rosenquist, *Up from the Ranks*, USA, 1961. Courtesy the estate of James Rosenquist

ANTIQUE POINTED EXTENDED.

A B C D E F G H I J K
L M N O P Q R S T U V
W X Y Z & .
1 2 3 4 5 6 7 8 9 0 .

ONE-HAND DEAF AND DUMB ALPHABET.

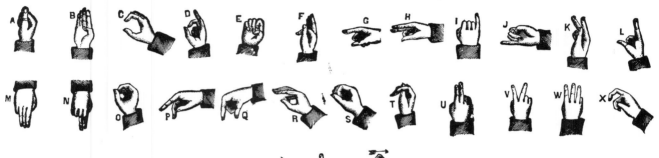

DORIC.

A B C D E F G H I J K L M N O P
Q R S T U V W X Y Z ?
a b c d e f g h i j k l m n o p q r s
t u v w x y z & $ 1 2 3 4 5 6 7 8 9 0 .

POINTED CONDENSED.

A B C D E F G H I J K L M N O P Q R S T
U V W X Y Z & $ 1 2 3 4 5 6 7 8 9 0 ? .

From a typefounders' manual, USA, c.1900

Refuge
The Ark

Death
Thumb Down (Nay)

Death
Black Swan

Education
Slate

Threat
Raised Fist

Failure
Dunce Cap

Correct
Hand Sign

Fame
Wreath and Trumpet

Correct
O.K.

Flop
Turkey

From a typefounders' manual, USA, c.1950

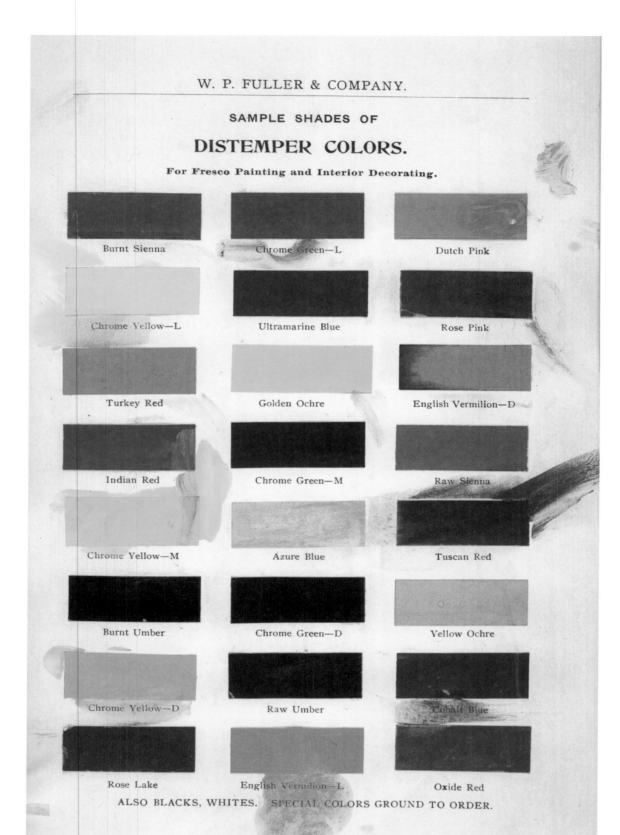

W. P. FULLER & COMPANY.

SAMPLE SHADES OF

DISTEMPER COLORS.

For Fresco Painting and Interior Decorating.

Burnt Sienna	Chrome Green—L	Dutch Pink
Chrome Yellow—L	Ultramarine Blue	Rose Pink
Turkey Red	Golden Ochre	English Vermilion—D
Indian Red	Chrome Green—M	Raw Sienna
Chrome Yellow—M	Azure Blue	Tuscan Red
Burnt Umber	Chrome Green—D	Yellow Ochre
Chrome Yellow—D	Raw Umber	Cobalt Blue
Rose Lake	English Vermilion—L	Oxide Red

ALSO BLACKS, WHITES.   SPECIAL COLORS GROUND TO ORDER.

Color sample chart, USA, late nineteenth century

Shaker "gift" drawing from *The Book of Prophetic Signs* by Prophet Isaiah, USA, 1843

ABCDEFG
HIJKLMN
OPQRST!
UVWXYZ
1234567
890&&?

Gothic Light, wood type, USA, c.1890

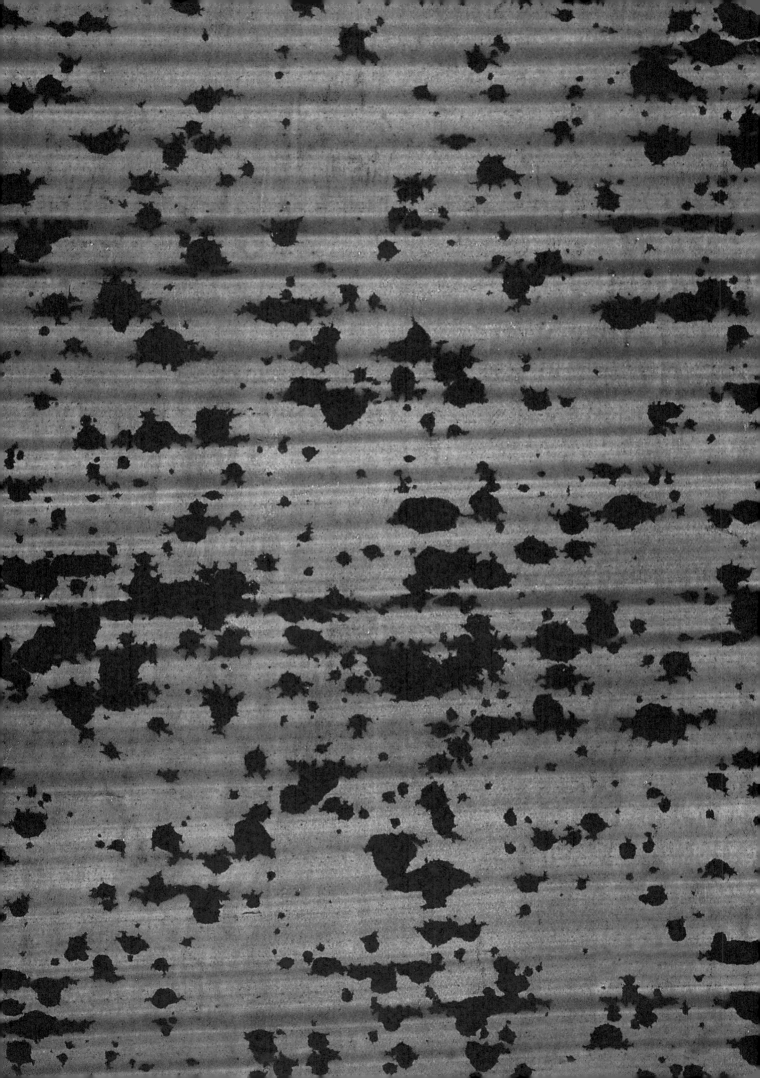

Poster, *Three Jazz Reviews*, designed by František Zelenka, Czechoslovakia, 1930

CZECH GRAPHIC MODERNISM

From early in the twentieth century, Czech writers, artists, architects, photographers, and designers were among the foremost modernists in Europe. In spite of the extreme limitations that were imposed on originality and artistic experimentation by the Communist Party of Czechoslovakia and its cultural agencies during the postwar period, the spirit of Czech modernism—inflected by a characteristic mix of melancholy and irony—survived, and indeed played a significant role in the resurgence of imaginative politics and culture that became the Velvet Revolution in 1989. Czech graphic modernism flowered in the 1920s and '30s, manifest especially in the astonishingly diverse invention of magazine, poster, book, and book-cover design that outmatched any comparable production elsewhere in the world. Its leading exponent was Karel Teige, the greatest of the Czech avant-garde artist-writers of the period.

Teige was responsible for the lettering design of the brilliant Abeceda (Alphabet) made in collaboration with the dancer Milča Mayerová and the poet Vítězslav Nezval. Using Karel Paspa's photographs of Mayerová, which contrive to be both erotic and chastely gymnastic, Teige's designs transform the alphabet into what is effectively a Constructivist manifesto: it proposes that gesture and pose are the living basis of semantics. The collaborators succeed in finding an utterly original and distinctive solution for every letter: Teige's brilliant alphabet of poses is animated into a graphic-visual dance, a stunning realization of the combination of photograph and lettering that László Moholy-Nagy termed "Typofoto." Nezval called it "a living poem."

Book cover; *The Baker Jan Marhoul* by Vladislav Vančura, designed by O. Mrkvička and Karel Teige, Czechoslovakia, 1924

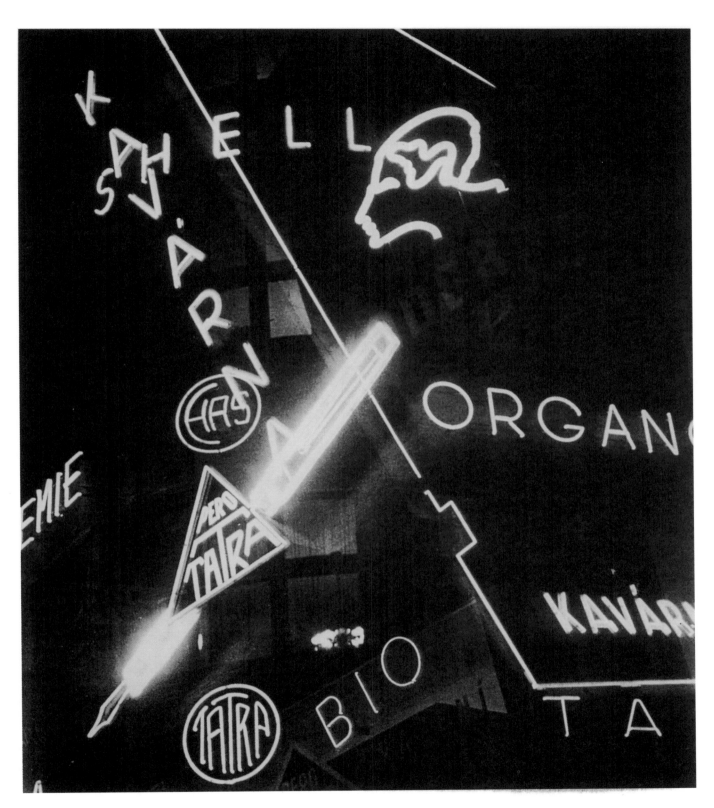

Jaromír Funke, *Neon Advertising*, Czechoslovakia, 1925

HNBDICRMKE

GOPÁVSYŮWL

JŠTZXFMYJQ

1234567890 2

abrphxfcvdn.

stgmjúyeikz

From *The Signwriters' Manual of Typefaces* by Richard Pípal, Czechoslovakia, 1956

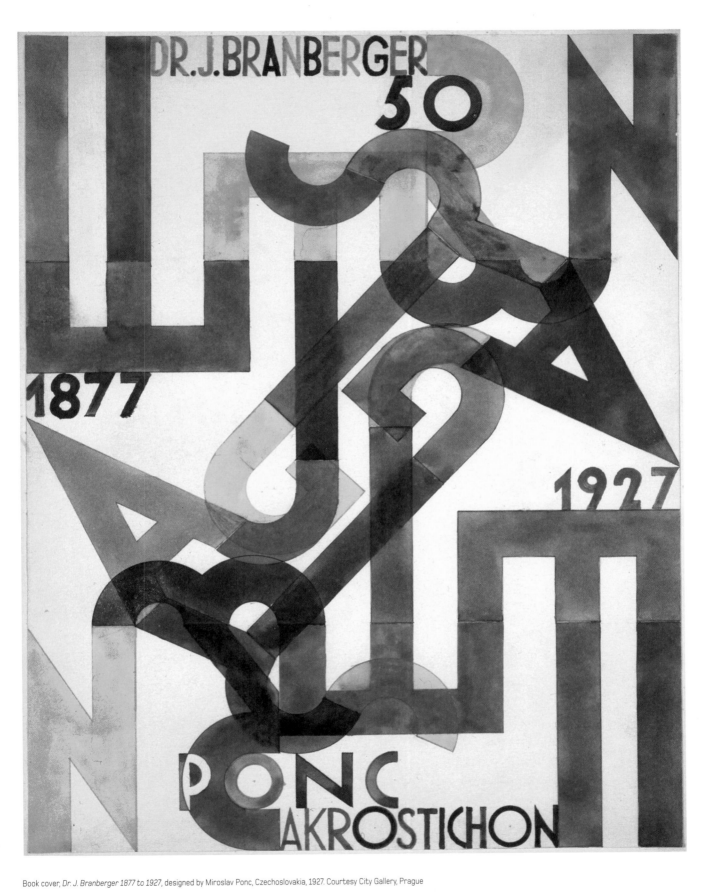

Book cover, *Dr. J. Branberger 1877 to 1927*, designed by Miroslav Ponc, Czechoslovakia, 1927. Courtesy City Gallery, Prague

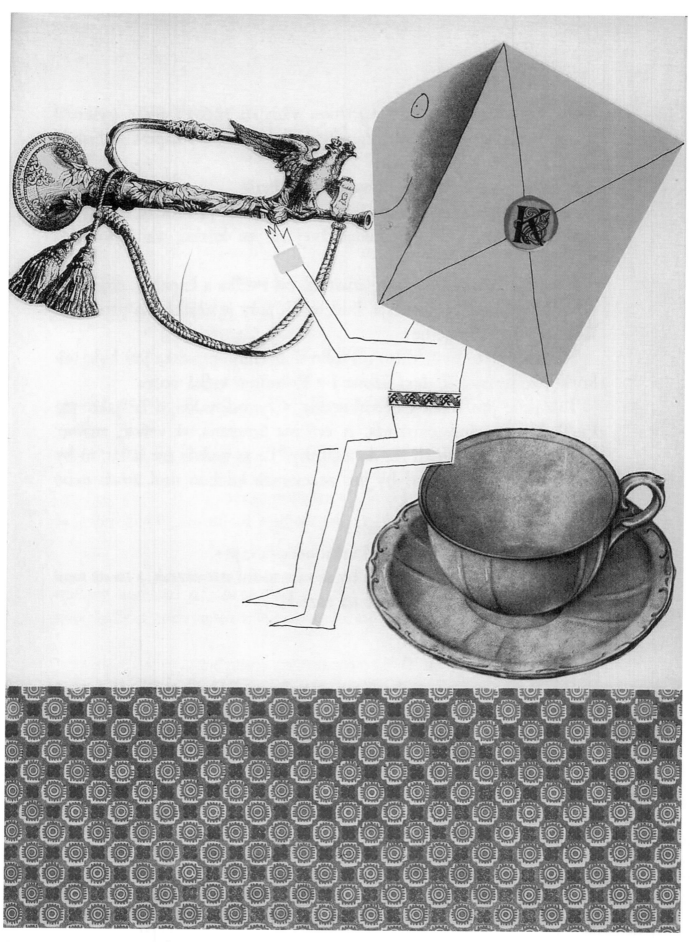

Illustration from *Crazy Fairy Tales* by Bohumil Štěpán, Czechoslovakia, 1965

HNBDIČRMKÉ
GOPAVSYUWL
JSTZXFMYJQ!,

1234567890:
abrphxfcvdn,
stgmjuyeikž

Typeface from *The Signwriters' Manual of Typefaces* by Richard Pípal, Czechoslovakia, 1956

ABCDEFGHIJ
KĽMNOPQRS
ŽÍ ŤTUVXYZW !?

PRÍLOHA 1
Pražský grotesk

АБВГЛЕДЕДЖЗИИК
ЛЛМНОПРСТУФХ
ЦЧШЩЭЮЯЁЫЬЪ

PRÍLOHA 2
Azbuka úzka

From *Methods of Lettering* by Fridrich Moravčík, Czechoslovakia, 1975

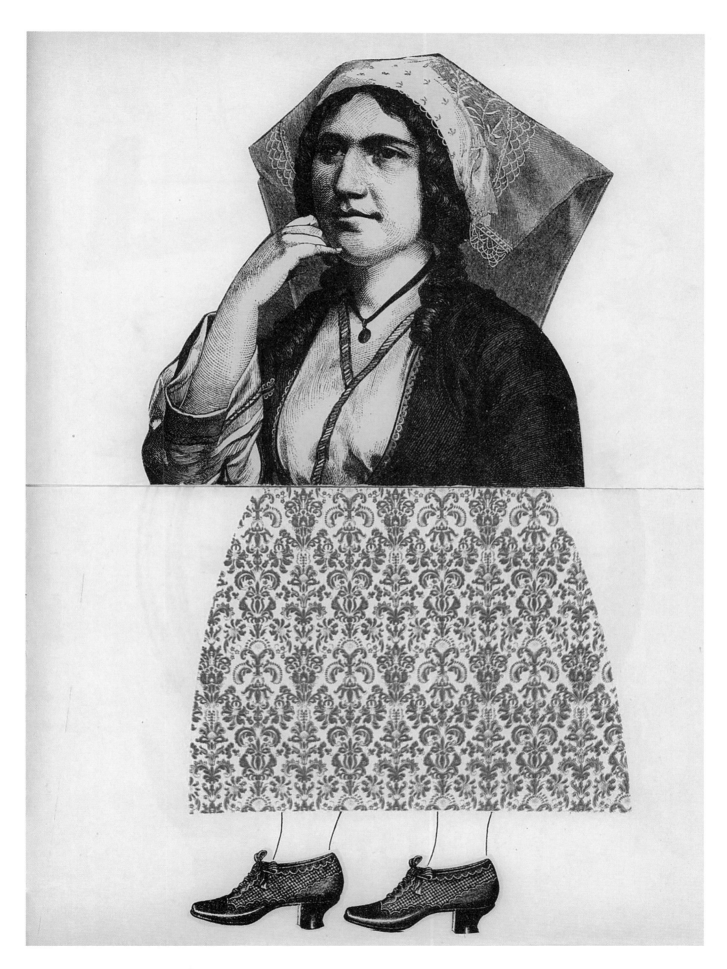

Illustration from *Crazy Fairy Tales* by Bohumil Štěpán, Czechoslovakia, 1965

Book cover, *Salukušky* by Ignát Herrmann designed by C. Bouda, Czechoslovakia, 1925

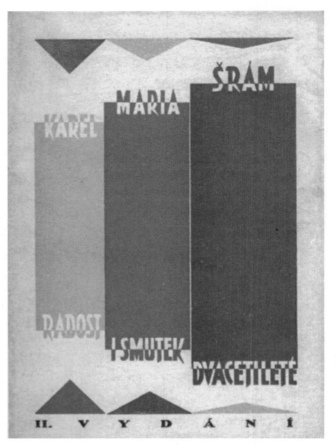

Book cover, *Joy and Sadness of a Twenty-Year-Old*, designed by K. M. Šrám, Czechoslovakia, 1925

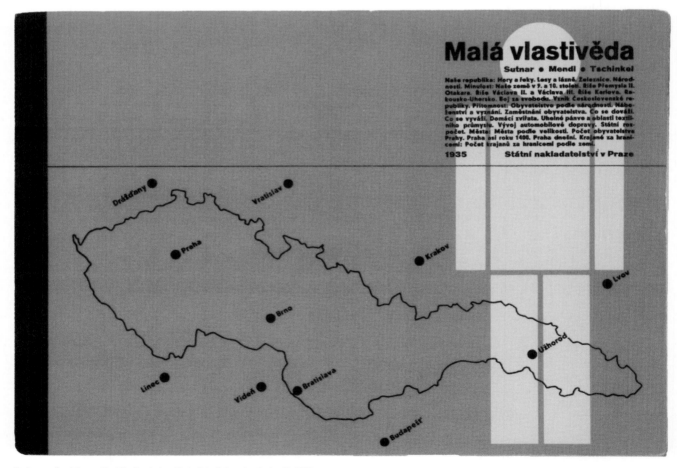

Book cover, *Small Geographical Studies*, designed by Ladislav Sutnar, Czechoslovakia, 1935

O 74

Logotypes from *The Typeface Handbook* by E. Beaufort, Czechoslovakia, c.1935. Courtesy Museum of Decorative Arts, Prague

ABCDEFGHIJKL
MPORSTUVVNWO
RJXYZVLTÁČĎĚÍ
ŇÝÓŘŠŤŮÚŽ=

1234567898₺₺₺=

abcdefghijklmno
pqrstuvuwxpyzáčď
ěěíňóřřšťúůpž

*₊↑//,,?!=→→↓↓

Typeface designed by Vojtěch Preissig, Czechoslovakia, 1914

Photograph by Josef Ehm, *Untitled*, Czechoslovakia, 1935

Book cover for *All Aboard for the Twentieth Century!* by Karel Teige, Czechoslovakia, 1928

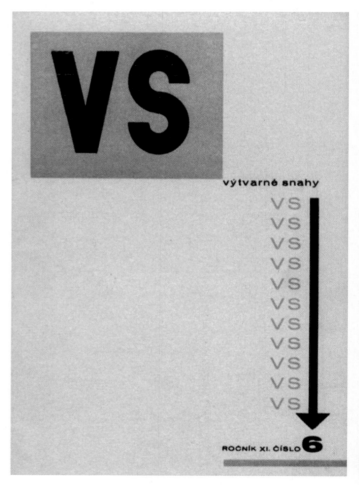

Book cover, *Artistic Efforts* by Výtvarné Snahy, designed by Ladislav Sutnar, Czechoslovakia, 1927

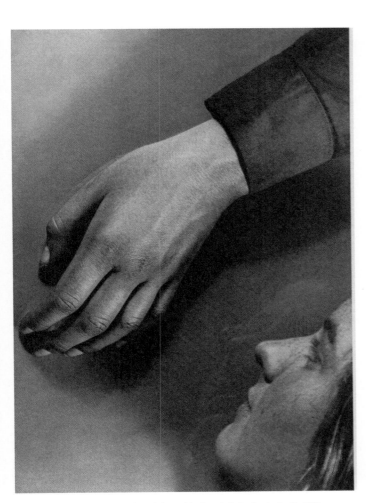

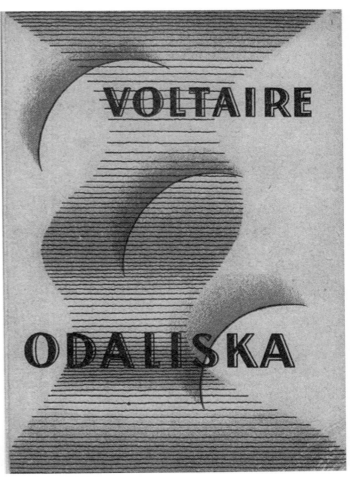

From *Photography Reflects the Surface*, photograph by Jaromír Funke, Czechoslovakia, 1935

Book cover, *Voltaire odaliska* by F. M. Arouet, designed by F. Zelenka, Czechoslovakia, 1928

HÁNOSŮĚBL
JDCKMPRW
ČVXZYIFT

nahebydskr
ctmfjópžgvl
wx2345678u

From *The Signwriters' Manual of Typefaces* by Richard Pipal, Czechoslovakia, 1956

Book cover for *Film Drama* by Louis Delluc, designed by Karel Teige, Czechoslovakia, 1928

Book cover, *Seated Woman* by Apollinaire, designed by Karel Teige and Otakar Mrkvička, Czechoslovakia, 1925

Book cover, *Diabolo* by Vitězslav Nezval, designed by Vit Orbel, Czechoslovakia, 1926

From *The Signwriters' Manual of Typefaces* by Richard Pipal, Czech Republic, 1956

Jazz Age alphabet by Karel Teige with Vítězslav Nezval, choreographed by the dancer Milča Mayerová, Czechoslovakia, 1926

Sheet music cover, *Aesop and Brabanec*, photomontage by F. Zelenka, Czechoslovakia, 1932

TAUCHNITZ EDITION

COLLECTION OF BRITISH AND AMERICAN AUTHORS

VOL. 5027

THE ENGLISH: ARE THEY HUMAN?

BY

G. J. RENIER

Carl Kravani
Wien ,7.
Mariahilferstraße 88a

LEIPZIG: BERNHARD TAUCHNITZ

PARIS: LIBRAIRIE GAULON & FILS, 39, RUE MADAME

Not to be introduced into the British Empire and U.S.A.

Book cover, *The English: Are They Human?* by G. J. Renier; unknown designer, Germany, 1932

Alphabet, *Enochian* (The Language of Angels), John Dee, England, late 16th century

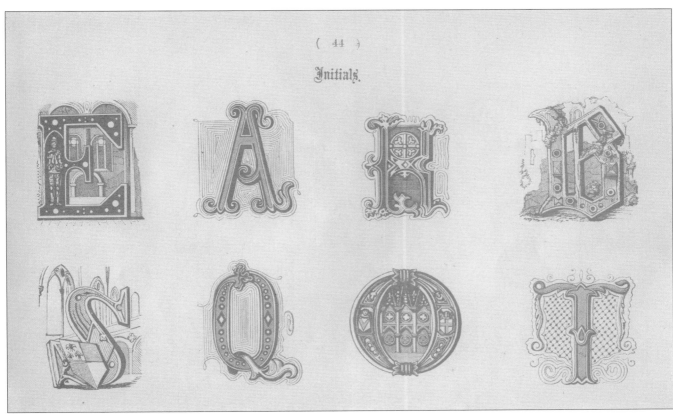

Initials, England, from the 15th and 16th centuries

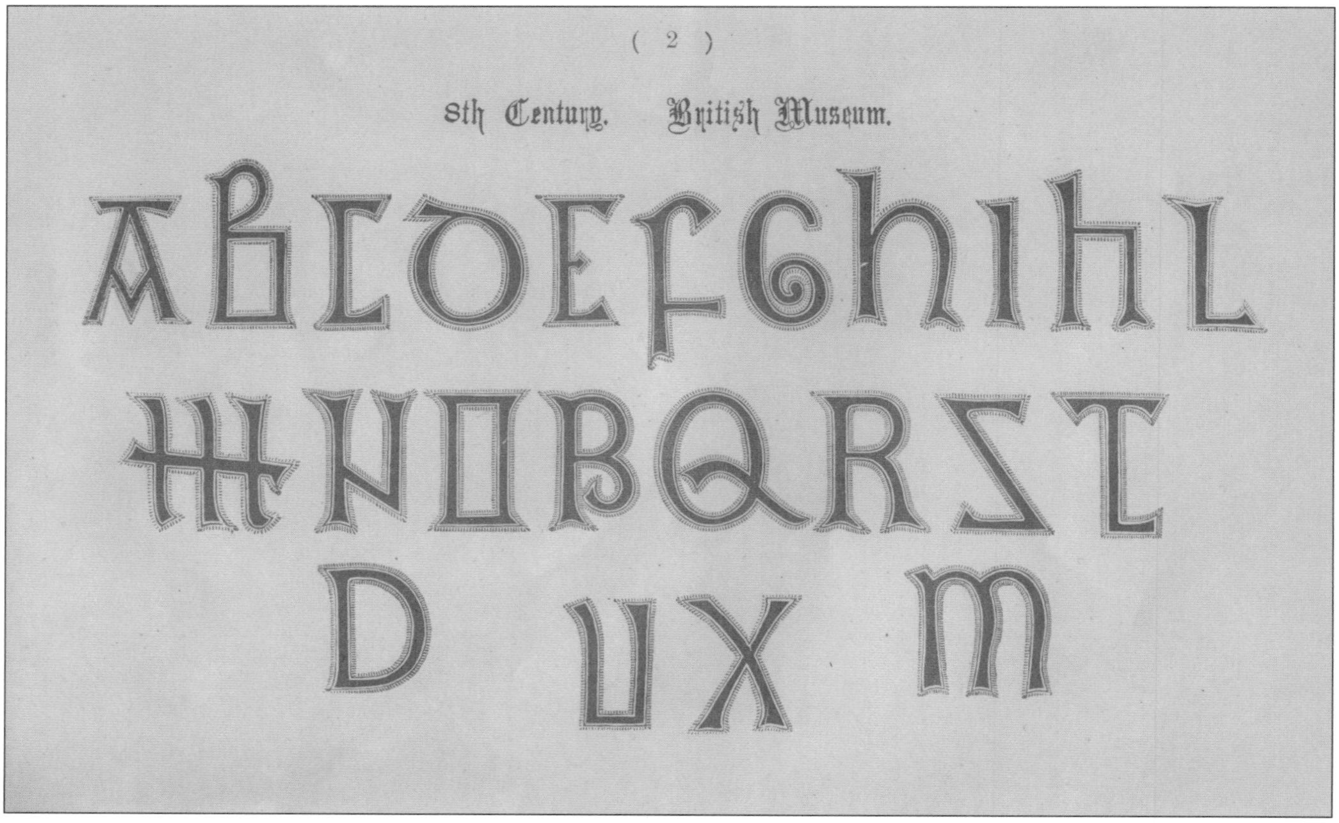

(2)

8th Century.   British Museum.

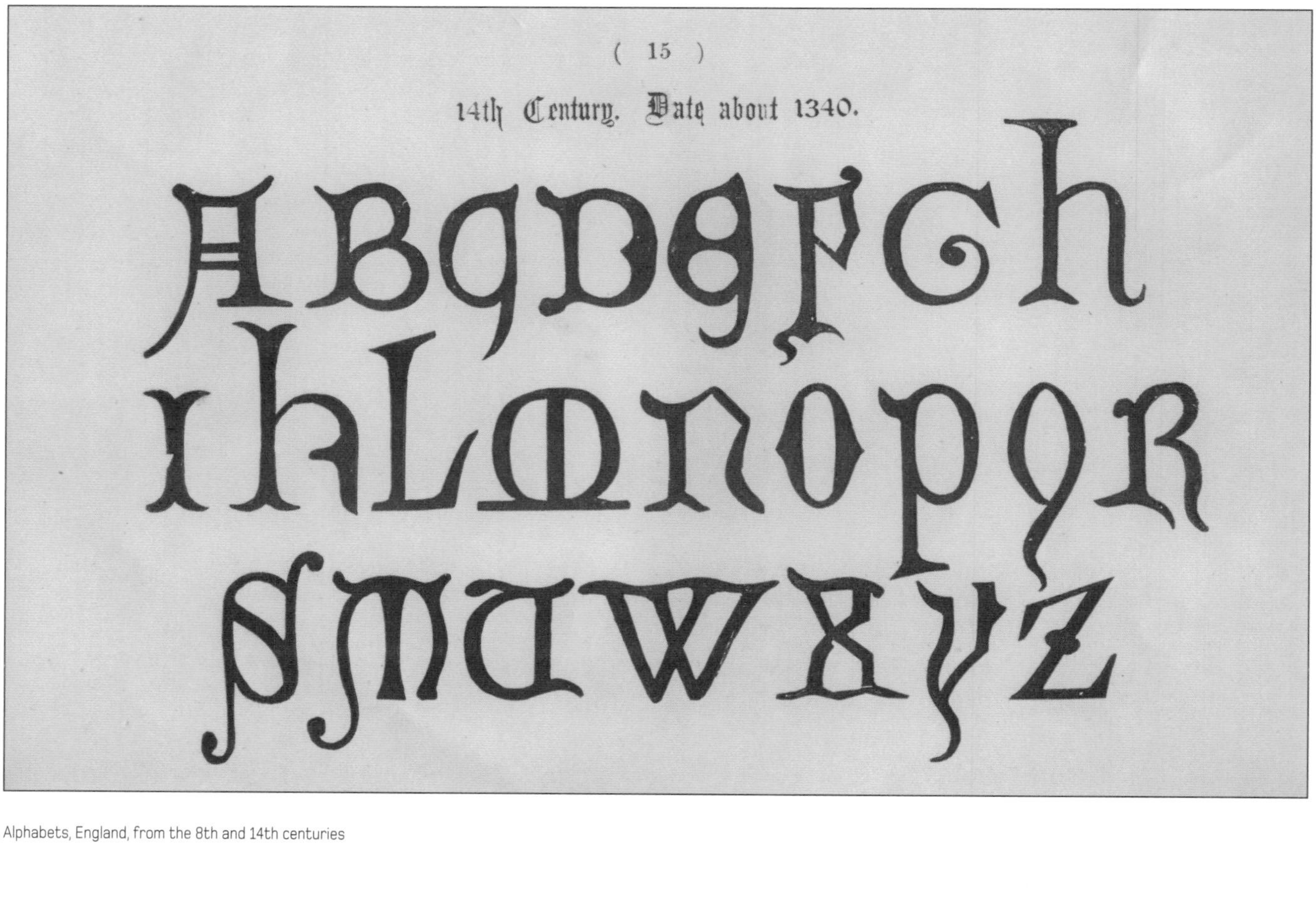

ABCDEFGHIHL
HNOBQRST
D UX M

(15)

14th Century. Date about 1340.

ABQDGFCh
IHLMNOPQR
SNUWXYZ

Alphabets, England, from the 8th and 14th centuries

86

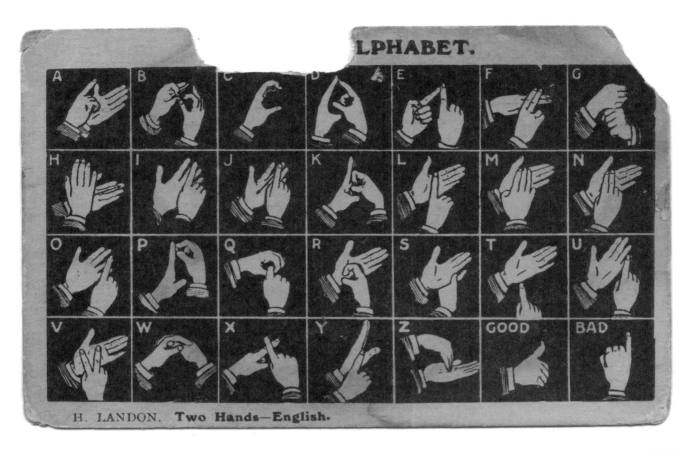

ALPHABET.

H. LANDON. **Two Hands—English.**

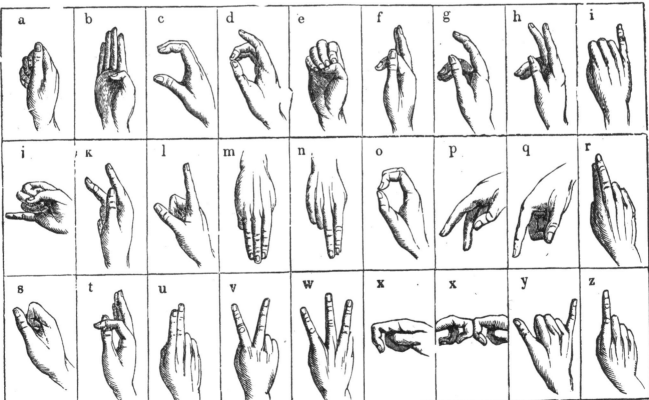

Sign language alphabets, UK, dates unknown

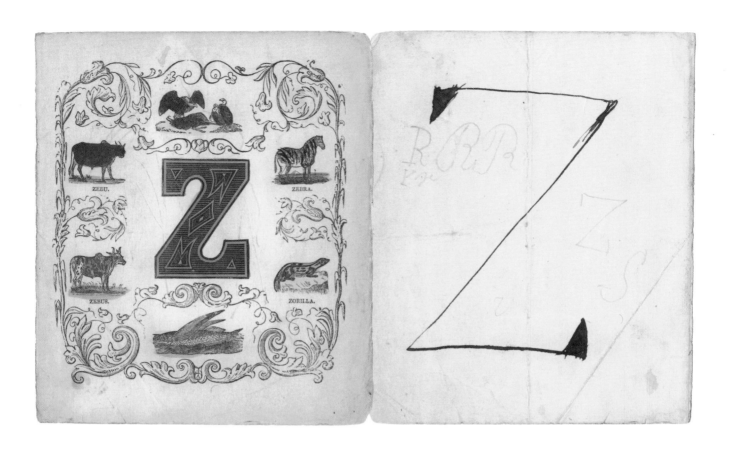

Marked pages from *The Panoramic Alphabet*, UK, 19th century. Courtesy Brian Webb collection

Shippers Box Marking

ABCDEFGHIJKL
MNOPQRSTUV
12345 WXYZ & 67890
abcddeffghijklmnopqrstuvwxyz

Fig. 34

Italic Script

ABCDEFGHIJKL
MNOPQRSTUV
WXYZ &
abcdefghijklmnopqrstuw
12345 wxyzz 67890

From a typefounders' catalogue, UK, 19th century. Courtesy Brian Webb collection

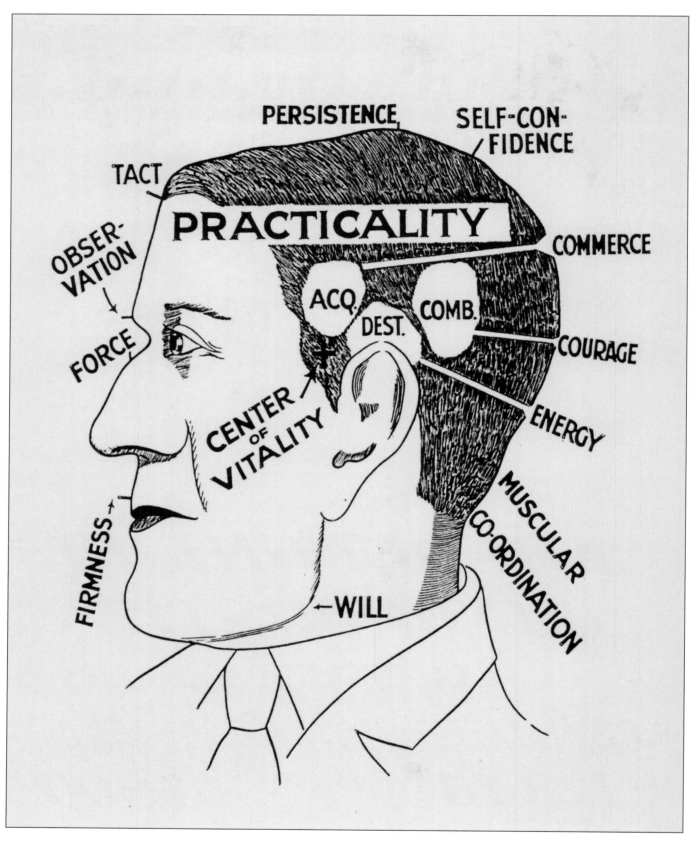

Phrenological head mapping the sites of faculties and characteristics, UK, 19th century

ABCDEFG
HIJKLMNO
PQRSTU
VWXYZ
.,;:'"!?-!?
£1234567
890&C°

From a typefounders' catalogue, UK, c.1940

Diamond Border No. 16

Diamond Border No. 14

Diamond Border No. 13

Diamond Border No. 15

DELITTLE'S DIAMOND BORDERS
for one or two colours.

By simply exchanging the first set of corners for a set as shown printed in blue, and which are included in every fount of 14 feet, the border is pushed into position for the second printing, and makes a very effective, handy and cheap two colour border. These borders are made in labour-saving lengths, and are all cut to one angle to join the corners. The number indicates both size and design.

Manufactured by
Robt. D. DELITTLE, Vine Street, York.

From the *Delittle Wood Type Catalogue*, UK, 1961. Courtesy Brian Webb collection

A B C D E F G H I J K L M N O P Q R S T U V W X

NOTE

For the remainder of this alphabet, points, figures, other characters, information, etc., see the following page

Typeface, *Ludlow Gothic Extra Condensed*, UK, c.1900

YZ&1234
567890$
£.:,,-'?!

Typeface, *Ludlow Gothic Extra Condensed*, UK, c.1900

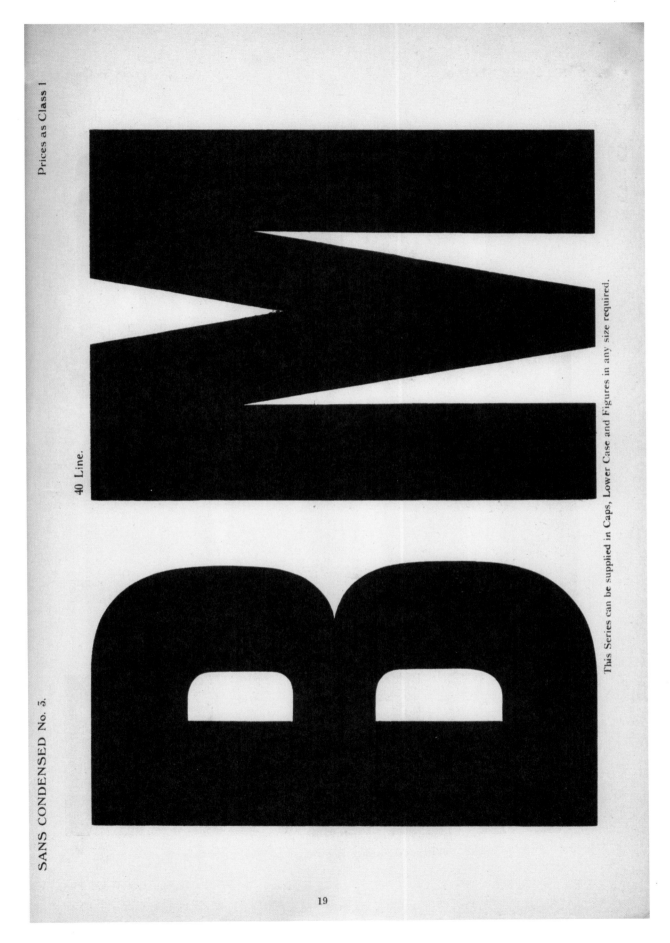

From the *Delittle Wood Type Catalogue*, UK, 1961. Courtesy Brian Webb collection

16 Line.

BRAID

30 Line.

RM

This Series can be supplied in Caps, Lower Case and Figures in any size required.

Machine Cut Wood Type

18

From the *Delittle Wood Type Catalogue*, UK, 1961. Courtesy Brian Webb collection

Photograph of the sun partially eclipsed, UK, 1914. Courtesy Michael Hoppen

surely endow her to be his wife.

17 If her father utterly refuſe to give her unto him, he ſhall pay money according to the dowry of virgins.

18 Thou ſhalt not ſuffer a witch to live. ✕ ✕ ✕ ✕

19 Whoſoever lieth with a beaſt ſhall ſurely be put to death. ✕ ✕ ✕ ✕ ✕

20 He that ſacrificeth unto any god ſave unto the LORD only, he ſhall be utterly deſtroyed. ✕ ✕ ✕

21 Thou ſhalt neither vex a ſtranger, nor oppreſs him: for ye were ſtrangers in the land of Egypt.

22 Ye ſhall not afflict any widow, or fatherleſs child.

23 If thou afflict them in any wiſe, and they cry at all unto me, I will ſurely hear their cry;

24 And my wrath ſhall wax hot, and I will kill you with the ſword; and your wives ſhall be widows, and your children fatherleſs.

25 If thou lend money to any of my people that is poor by thee, thou ſhalt not be to him as an uſurer, neither ſhalt thou lay upon him uſury.

26 If thou at all take thy neighbour's raiment to pledge, thou ſhalt deliver it unto him by that the ſun goeth down:

27 For that is his covering only, it is his raiment for his ſkin: wherein ſhall he ſleep? and it ſhall come to paſs, when he crieth unto me, that I will hear; for I am gracious.

28 Thou ſhalt not revile the gods, nor curſe the ruler of thy people.

29 Thou ſhalt not delay to offer the firſt of thy ripe fruits, and of thy liquors: the firſtborn of thy ſons ſhalt thou give unto me.

30 Likewiſe ſhalt thou do with thine oxen, and with thy ſheep: ſeven days it ſhall be with his dam; on the eighth day thou ſhalt give it me.

From *The Macklin Bible* with text highlighted by Alfred Woods, UK, 1888–1900. Courtesy David Batterham

ABCDEFI
GHJKLM
NOPQRW
STUVYXZ

From a typefounders' catalogue, UK, mid-19th century

abcdefg
hijklno
mpqrſw
stuvxyz

From a typefounders' catalogue, UK, mid-19th century

From *Plouf, The Little Wild Duck* illustrated by Rojan, UK, 1936

abdeghk
npqe vv
nw dos
xyzfijrtl

Typeface by Edward Wright, UK, 1965. Courtesy the Department of Typography and Graphic Communication at the University of Reading

Pavel Büchler, *The Critic*, UK, 2001

ABCDEFG
HIJKLMN
OPQRSTU
VWXYZ&!

abcdefghijklmn
opqrstuvwxyz!

123456789

From a typefounders' catalogue, UK, mid-19th century

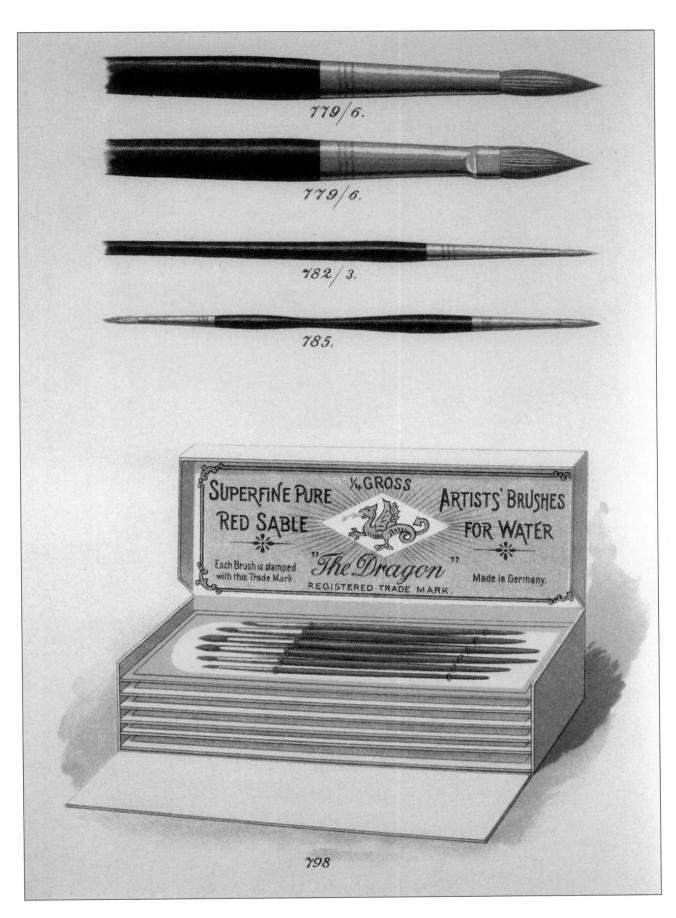

779/6.

779/6.

782/3.

785.

SUPERFINE PURE
RED SABLE
¼ GROSS
ARTISTS' BRUSHES
FOR WATER

"The Dragon"
REGISTERED TRADE MARK.

Each Brush is stamped
with this Trade Mark.

Made in Germany.

798

From a trade catalogue, UK, c.1895

Poster designed by E. McKnight Kauffer, *Air Mail*, UK, 1935. © Simon Rendall

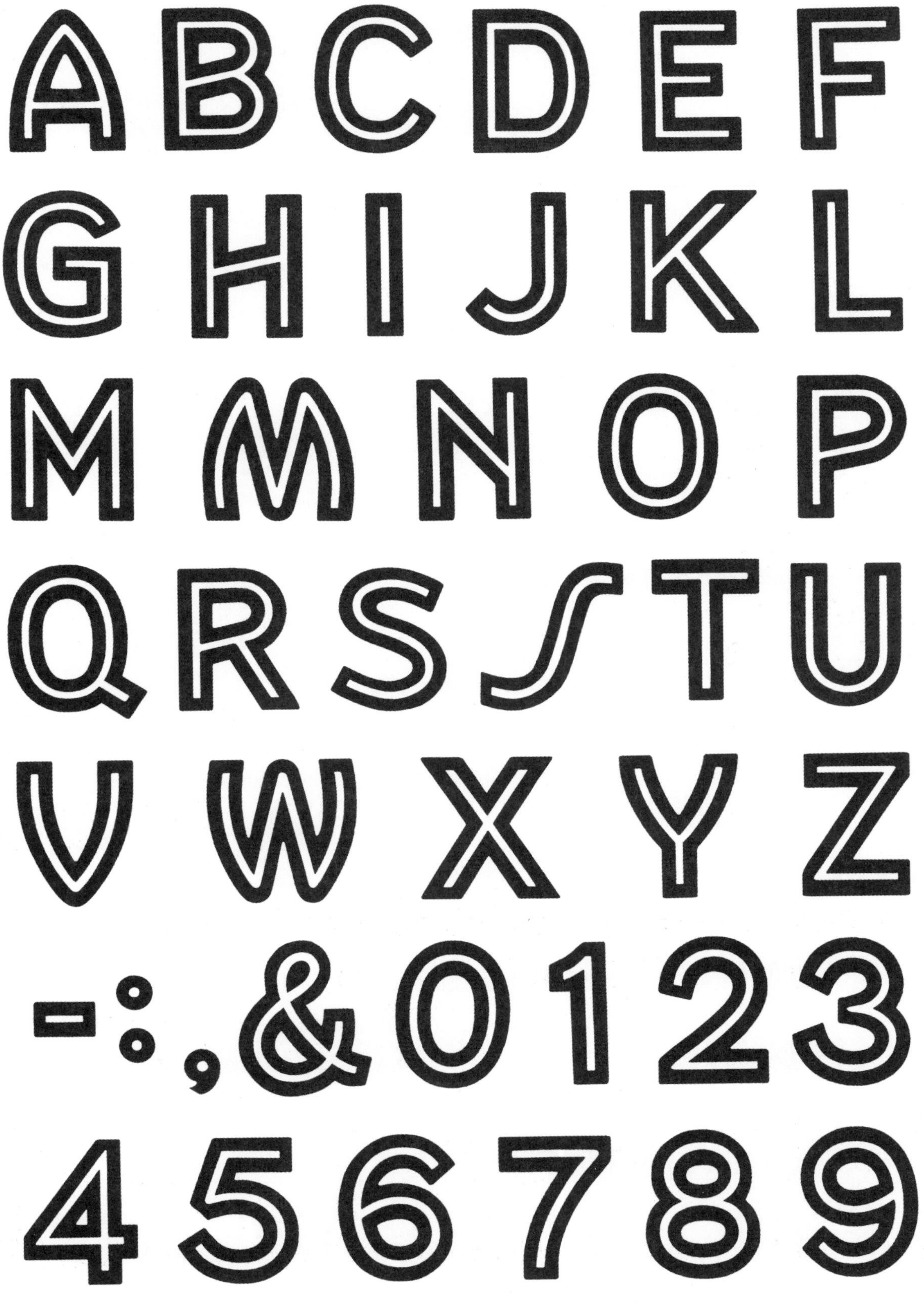

ABCDEF
GHIJKL
MMNOP
QRSSTU
VWXYZ
-:,&0123
456789

Hand-drawn alphabet by Richard Hollis, UK, 1989

CHAPTER II.

THE FIRST SABBATH. GARDEN OF EDEN. TREE OF KNOWLEDGE. NAMES OF THE CREATURES. THE MAKING OF WOMAN; AND INSTITUTION OF MARRIAGE.

Thus the heavens and the earth were finished, and all the host of them.

2 And on the seventh day God ended his work which he had made; and he rested on the seventh day from all his work which he had made.

3 And God blessed the seventh day, and sanctified it: because that in it he had rested from all his work which God created and made.

The art of lay-out nowadays owes its strength to its free use of processes. From photographic apparatus, scissors, a bottle of Indian ink, a gum-pot, combined with the hand of the designer and an unprejudiced eye, a composition can be evolved and a novel idea expressed by simple means.

Pages 111–116 from *Mise en Page, The Theory and Practice of Lay-out* by A. Tolmer, UK, 1932

THE THEORY AND PRACTICE OF LAYOUT

In 1932 the *Studio* magazine published *Mise en Page, The Theory and Practice of Lay-out* by A. Tolmer. The genius of the booklet was to instruct by example, and its texts were models of modernist economy and grace. It sought to inculcate the virtues of simplicity, balance, clarity of expression, and freedom from preconceptions with regard to the use of materials and processes. Apart from its exemplary value as a design manual, what gives *Mise en Page* an undeniable poignancy is its conviction: the necessity to civilized life of principled thought and humane feeling in good printing practice. For Tolmer, as for Wittgenstein, it seems that "ethics and aesthetic are one."

Like skating or walking the tight-rope, the art of lay-out is an art of balance.

It cannot however be expressed merely as a mathematical calculation. The tight-rope walker steadies herself with her parasol rather than with the aid of a formula. The sense of stability; the right and the wrong way of doing anything; the amount of air that enables the earth to breathe; the amount of sleep that permits of the greatest activity during the day; the most satisfactory way of combining the elements of a theatre-set, the page of a book or a poster; all these things are essentially a matter of feeling.

The feelings of mankind are unaffected by the change of ideas, constructive and destructive by turns, which accompany each phase of history. Since the earliest times known to us, love, hate, joy, suffering and religion have exercised a constant influence. Every age and every civilization, therefore, must be guided by these basic impulses and the works produced under their influence, in order to test, control, and correct its own balance.

So, considering the past, we might have written simply an historical study of the kind of balance represented by the art of lay-out. But this we have wished to avoid. If an historical evolution may be traced in the series of illustrations here reproduced it will not be by any means complete.

An investigation has been made into the origins of the art of lay-out. The part played by the shape of text in a lay-out has been demonstrated by reference to various types of ancient writing. The links between letterpress, ornament, and architecture have been pointed out. Points of comparison between modes of lay-out used in different countries and at different periods have been established. The sole aim, however, has been that of providing rich materials for the modern method of approach.

It is always a difficult matter for the professional tennis-player to discuss his game. But this is not a series of lessons in lay-out. We wish to immerse our readers in the subject and to prime them with information which will enable them to infuse fresh life and a continually changing novelty into their practice of it.

There is no technique of which modern publicity has not made use. Arrangements of cut-outs and cut paper have given a new direction to photographic advertising. We shall soon be seeing three-dimensional posters on the hoadings.

Photography gives concrete form to the subtlest thoughts. It has the gift of imparting to the dullest, most mechanical and impersonal things the sensitiveness and poetry which admits them into our dreams.

From *The Next Call* by H. N. Werkman, the Netherlands, c.1924. Courtesy Brian Webb collection

Typeface, Condensed Grotesque designed by Joost Schmidt, with construction details and variants of single figures, upper- and lowercase, the Netherlands, 1926. Courtesy Richard Hollis

Alphabet designed by André Vlaanderen, the Netherlands, 1928

From *The Next Call* by H. N. Werkman, the Netherlands, c.1924. Courtesy Brian Webb collection

4

A B C D E F
G H I J K L M
N O P Q R S T
U V W X Y Z

Rotterdamsche Schilderschool.
A. R. VAN DER BURG.

A. R. VAN DER BURG.

6

a b c d e f g h i
j k l m n o p q r s
t u v w x i j y z
1 2 3 4 5 6 7 8 9 0

Rotterdamsche Schilderschool.
A. R. VAN DER BURG.

A. R. VAN DER BURG.

Signwriters' alphabet, from the *Rotterdamsche Schilderschool*, compiled by A. R. van der Burg, the Netherlands, early 1900s. Courtesy Jan Tholenaar Collection

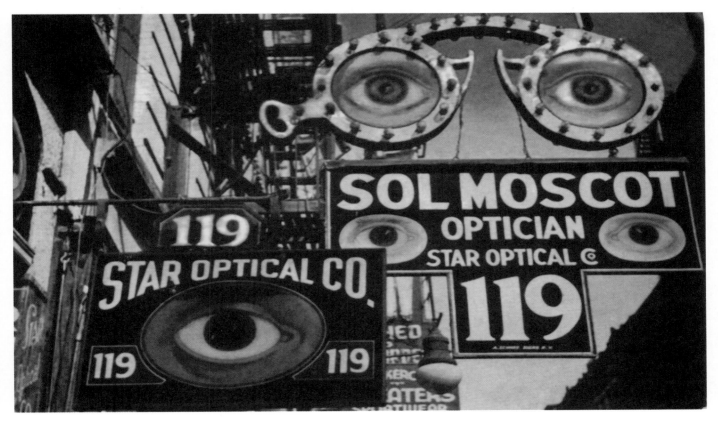

Optician's shop signs, Orchard Street, New York, USA, 1935

DIAGNOSTIC EYE CHARTS

Eye charts using letters of the alphabet, designed to test visual acuity and the efficacy of corrective lenses, were first introduced in the 1830s. To increase optical distance in the testing room, some charts were designed with reversed letters and viewed through a facing mirror. In 1862 the Utrecht optometrist Herman Snellen designed the first scientifically reliable charts for testing vision distance, using carefully size-adjusted letters based on the typeface Paragon Egyptian. Sans serif letters, having less visual distraction, were introduced soon after. (Gills Sans Bold has been especially popular with British ophthalmic opticians.) In the 1870s Snellen introduced charts with calibrated lines and abstract figures for young or illiterate patients. Eye chart designs all over the world are still based on Snellen's pioneering charts, called Optotypes. The economy and clarity demanded by its function gave the eye chart a typographic formal elegance that was modernist *avant la lettre*.

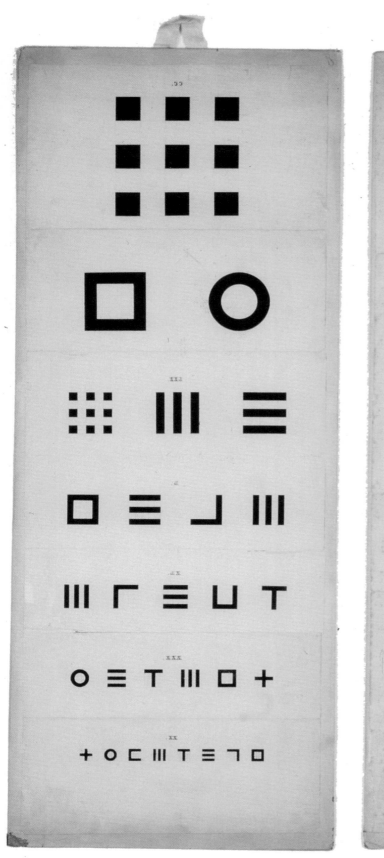 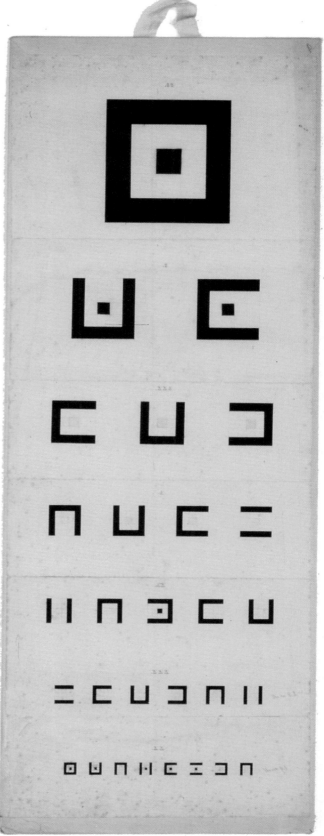

Snellen eye charts for non-readers, the Netherlands, 1996. Courtesy of BV Uitgeverij De Bataafsche Leeuw, Van Soeren and Co., Amsterdam

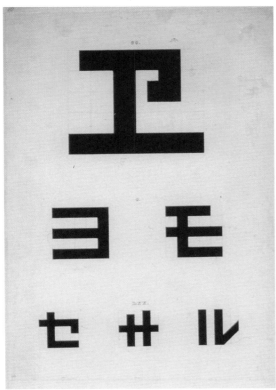

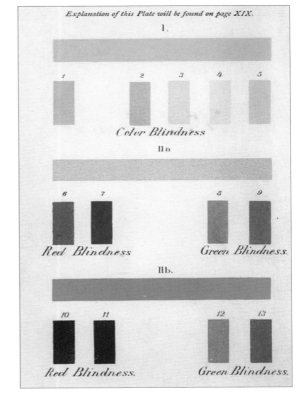

Early eye test and color blindness charts, mid-19th century

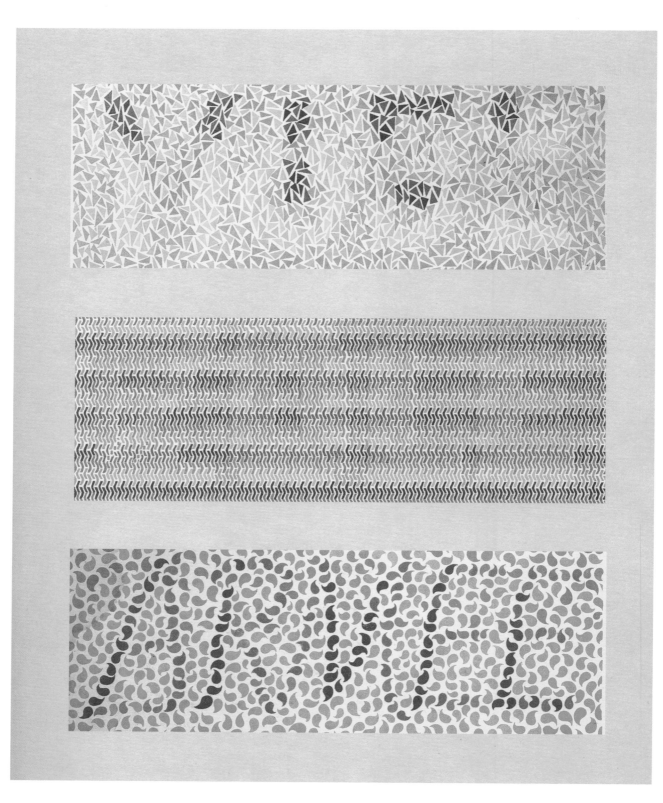

H. Podesta, color blindness test, Germany, 1916

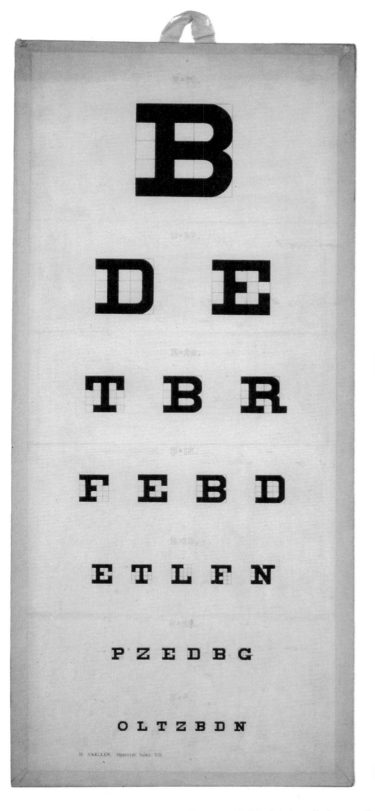
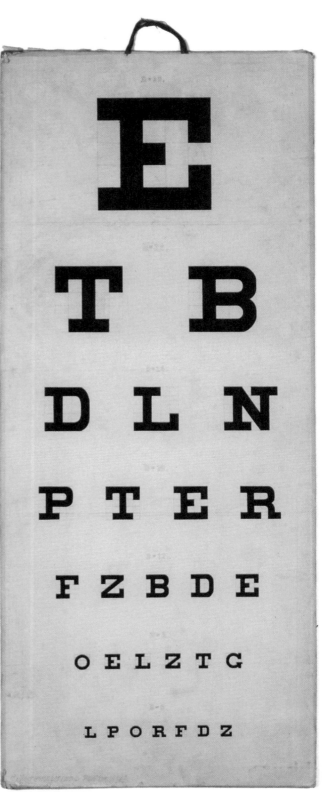

Snellen eye charts, the Netherlands, 1996. Courtesy of BV Uitgeverij De Bataafsche Leeuw, Van Soeren and Co., Amsterdam

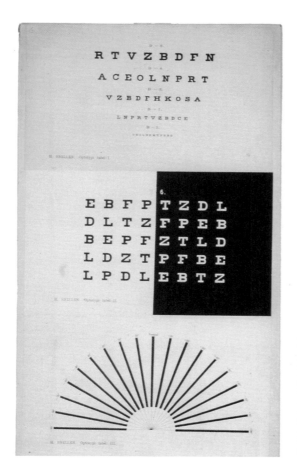

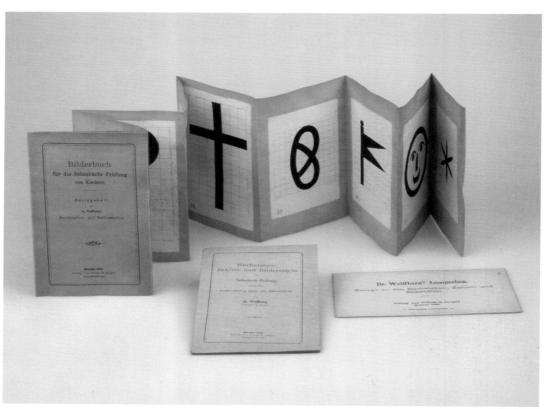

Eye charts, the Netherlands, 1996. Courtesy of BV Uitgeverij De Bataafsche Leeuw, Van Soeren and Co., Amsterdam

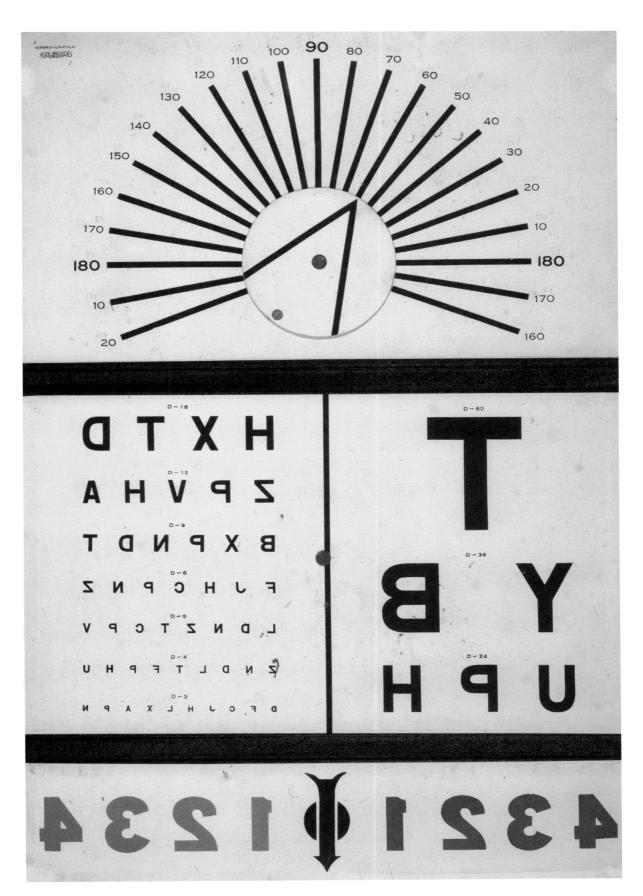

Eye chart, UK, date unkown

Joan Brossa-*Poema visual*

Visual Poem, Joan Brossa, Spain, 1978. Courtesy Fundació Joan Brossa

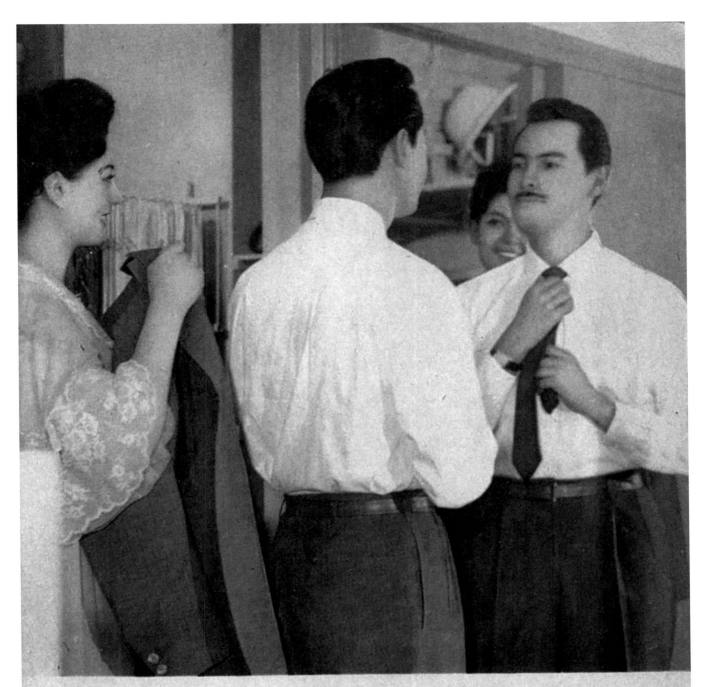

PARA SUS FIESTAS...

Goce con LIBERTAD DE ACCION

La Camisa CLOVER reúne todo: CALIDAD • AMPLITUD • ELEGANCIA • Y EXCLUSIVIDAD EN TODOS SUS DISEÑOS. Además, Cortos y Pantalones CLOVER.

Camisas

Clover

Línea de Oro

Y PARA SUS HIJOS, CAMISAS Y PANTALONES *Cadete*

CC-8/60

Advertisement for Camisas Clover, *Reader's Digest*, Mexico, 1960

137

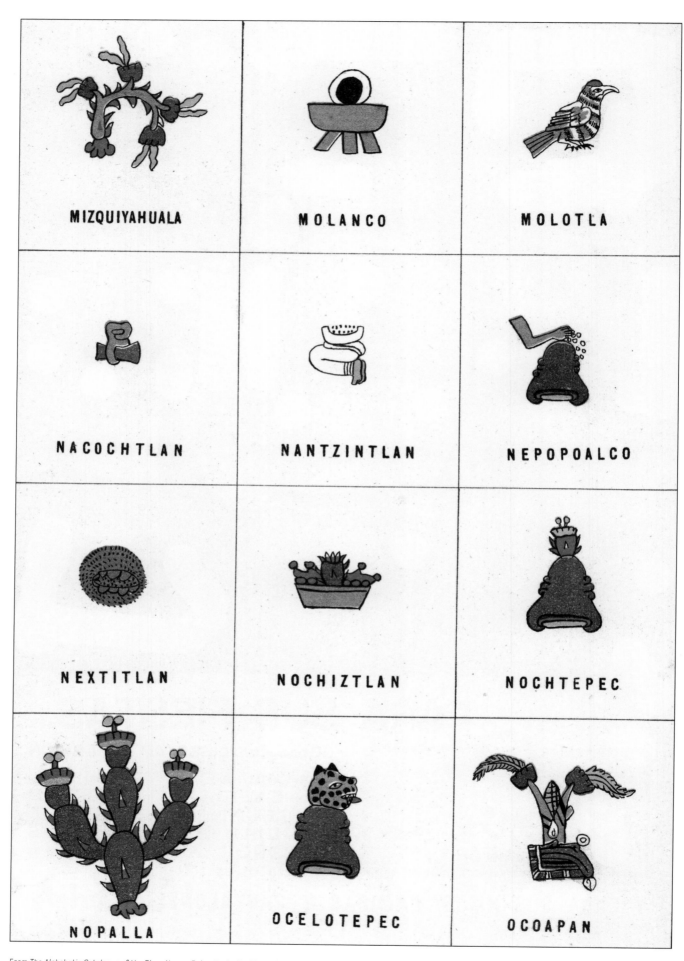

MIZQUIYAHUALA

MOLANCO

MOLOTLA

NACOCHTLAN

NANTZINTLAN

NEPOPOALCO

NEXTITLAN

NOCHIZTLAN

NOCHTEPEC

NOPALLA

OCELOTEPEC

OCOAPAN

From *The Alphabetic Catalogue of the Place Names Belonging to the Nahuatl Language* by Antonio Peñafiel, Mexico, 1885. Courtesy Pablo Butcher

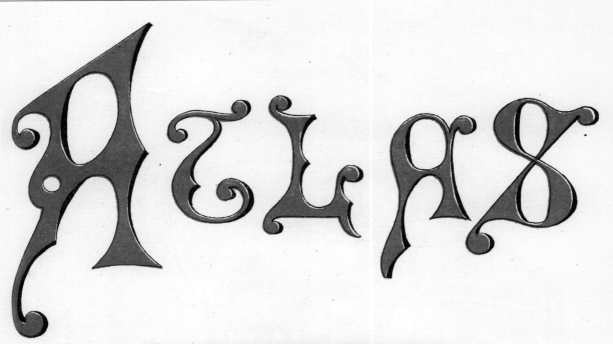

IMP, Y LIT, ESPAÑOLA

MÉXICO.

MDCCCLXXXV.

Print for Day of the Dead, *The Alcoholic Calavera* by J. G. Posada, Mexico, 1866

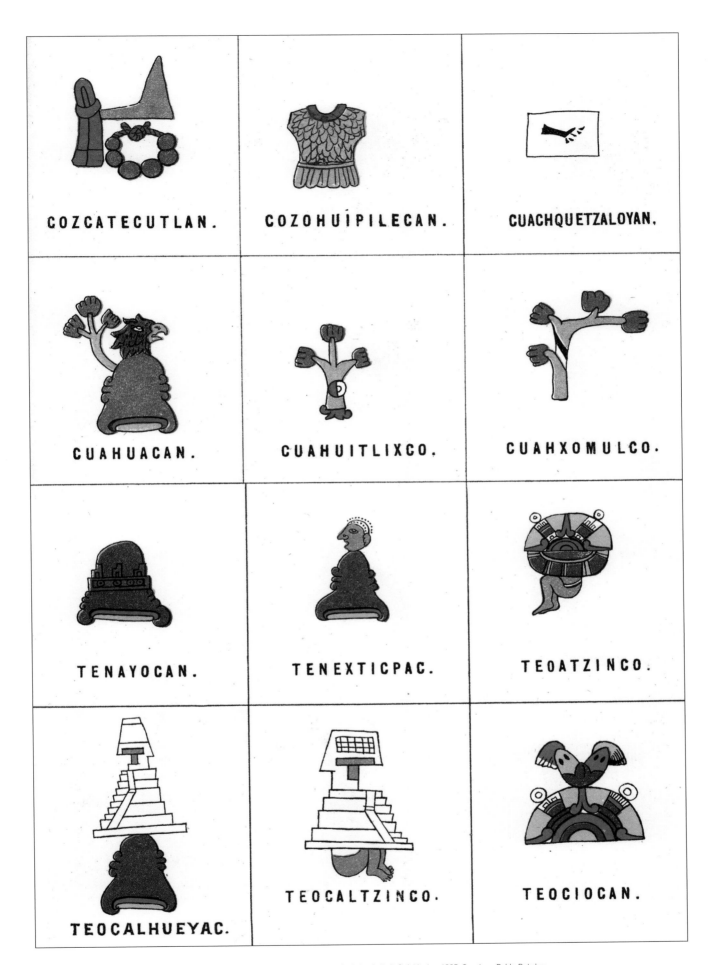

COZCATECUTLAN.

COZOHUÍPILECAN.

CUACHQUETZALOYAN.

CUAHUACAN.

CUAHUITLIXCO.

CUAHXOMULCO.

TENAYOCAN.

TENEXTICPAC.

TEOATZINCO.

TEOCALHUEYAC.

TEOCALTZINCO.

TEOCIOCAN.

From *The Alphabetic Catalogue of the Place Names Belonging to the Nahuatl Language* by Antonio Peñafiel, Mexico, 1885. Courtesy Pablo Butcher

Poster, *Household Objects*, Mexico, c.1950

Magazine cover, *Sinopsis,* designed by Miguel Prieto, Mexico, 1953. Courtesy Xavier Bermúdez

Abecedario

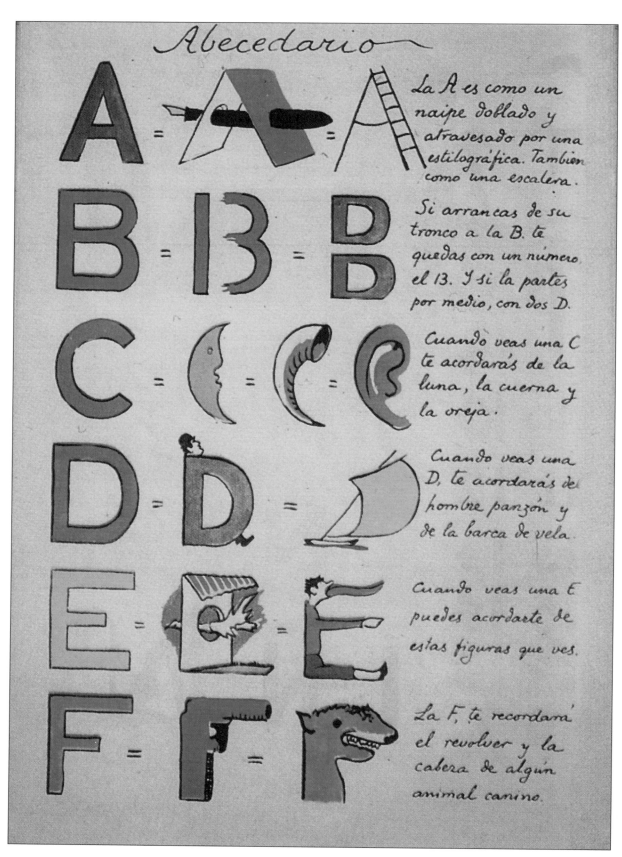

A = A = A

La A es como un naipe doblado y atravesado por una estilográfica. También como una escalera.

B = B = D D

Si arrancas de su tronco a la B, te quedas con un número, el 13. Y si la partes por medio, con dos D.

C = C = C

Cuando veas una C te acordarás de la luna, la cuerna y la oreja.

D = D =

Cuando veas una D, te acordarás del hombre panzón y de la barca de vela.

E = E = E

Cuando veas una E puedes acordarte de estas figuras que ves.

F = F =

La F, te recordará el revólver y la cabeza de algún animal canino.

From *What My Parrot Knew* by José Moreno Villa, Mexico, 1945

¡CASO RARO!

UNA MUJER QUE DIO A LUZ
TRES NIÑOS
Y CUATRO ANIMALES.

Newspaper illustration, *Rare Case! A Woman Who Gave Birth to Three Children and Four Animals* by J. G. Posada, Mexico, c.1865

Book cover for *Cobra Norato* by Raul Bopp, designed by Flavio de Carvalho, Brazil, 1931

Book cover and woodcut for *Urbe* by Manuel Maples Arce, illustrated by Jean Charlot, Mexico, 1924

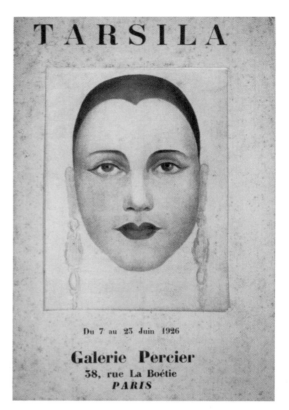

Book cover, *Paulicea Desvairada*, designed by Alvaro Moya, Brazil, 1922

Catalogue cover, designed by Tarsilo do Amiral, Brazil, 1926

Book cover, *Pau Brasil* by Oswald de Andrade, designed by Tarsila do Amaral, Brazil, 1925

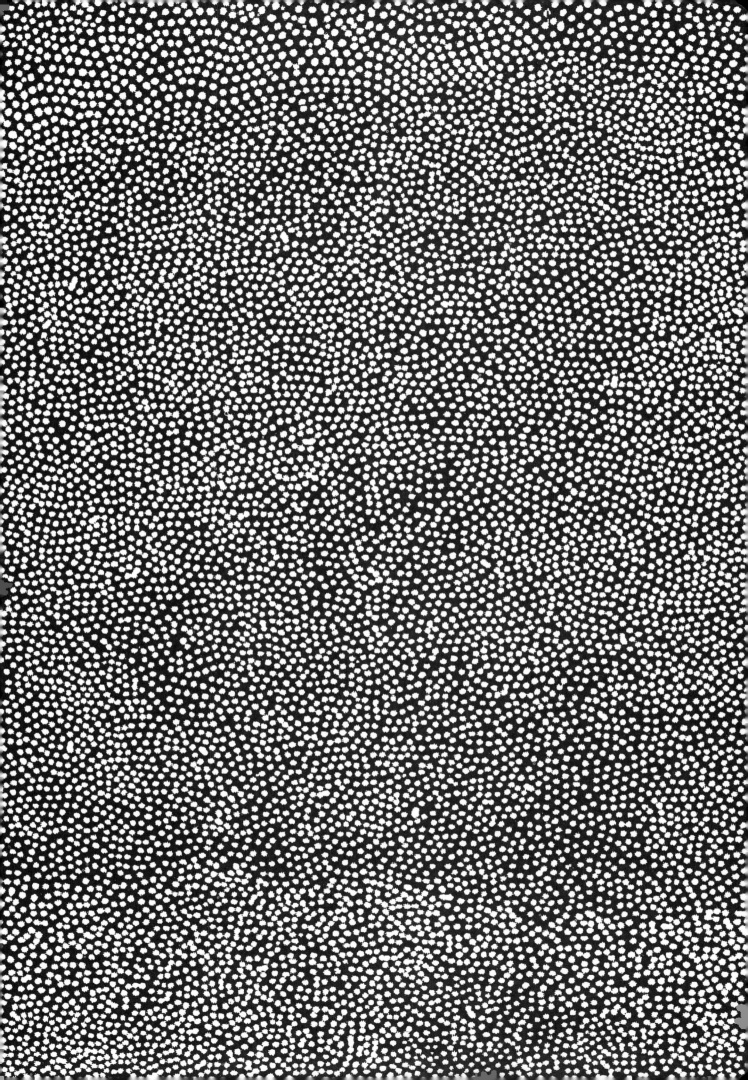

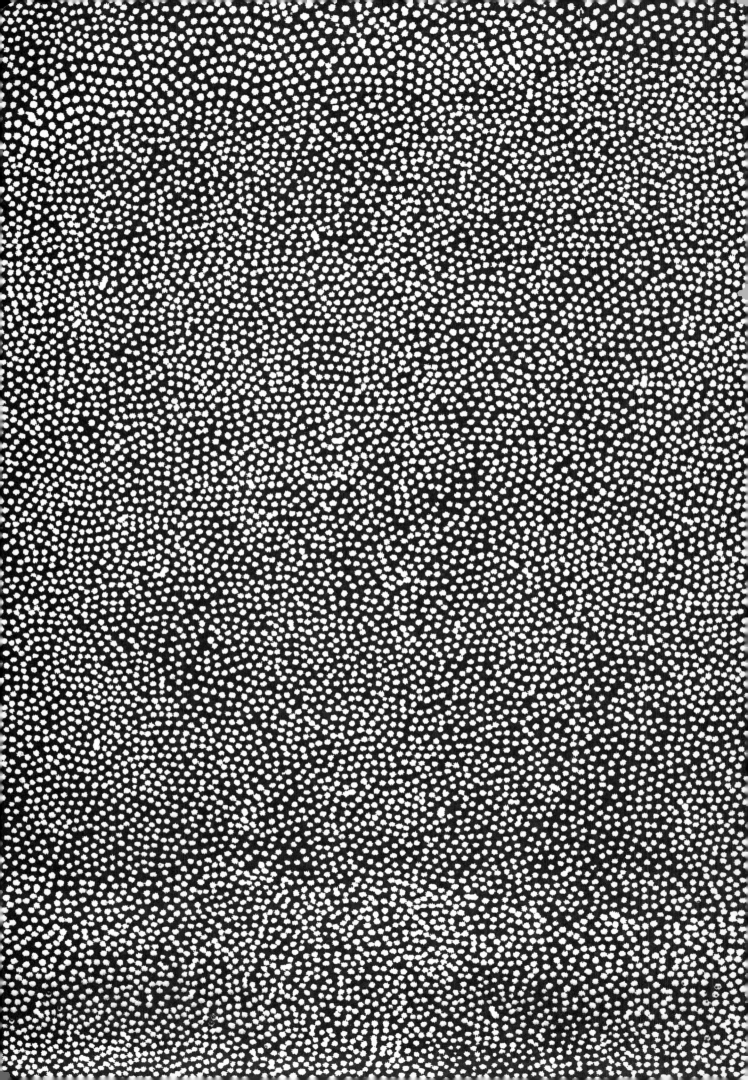

Poster, *The Picture of the Year: Red Russia,* designed by B. Aronson, Russia, 1923

Sketches for shop signs by Nikolai Suetin, USSR, 1921

А Б В Г

Д Е Ж З И

К Л М Н О

П Р С Т У Ф Х

Ц Ч Ш Щ

Ъ Ь Ю Я

---

1 2 3 4 5 6 7

8 9 & 9 0

Russian block alphabet, designer and date unknown. Courtesy David Hillman

El Lissitzky, flag stands for the Soviet pavilion at the *Pressa* exhibition, USSR, 1928

El Lissitzky, *Old Man (Head 2 Steps Behind)*, Russia, c.1920

ČTYŘCICERO „PATRONA" GROTESK RUSKÉ

АБВГДЕЖЗИ

| A | БВ | BV | ГG | ДD | E | ЖŽ | ЗZ | ИI | I |

ЙКЛМНОПРС

| ЙJ | К | ЛL | M | НN | O | ПР | PR | CS |

ТУФХЦЧШЩЪ

| T | УU | ФF | ХCH | ЦC | ЧČ | ШŠ | ЩŠČ | Ъ |

ЫЬѢЭЮЯѲѴ

| ЫY | Ь | Ѣ | ЭE | ЮJU | ЯJA | ѲF | Ѵ I neb Y |

ЉЊЋЂЈЏЖЉ

| ЉLJ | ЊŇ | Ћ † | ЂĐ | J | Џ DŽ | Ж A | Љ JA |

━━━━━━━━━━━━

В.А. ФРАНЦЕВЪ

ПРАГА

Russian version of *Patrona Grotesk* typeface, Czechoslovakia, c.1930. Courtesy Jan Solpera

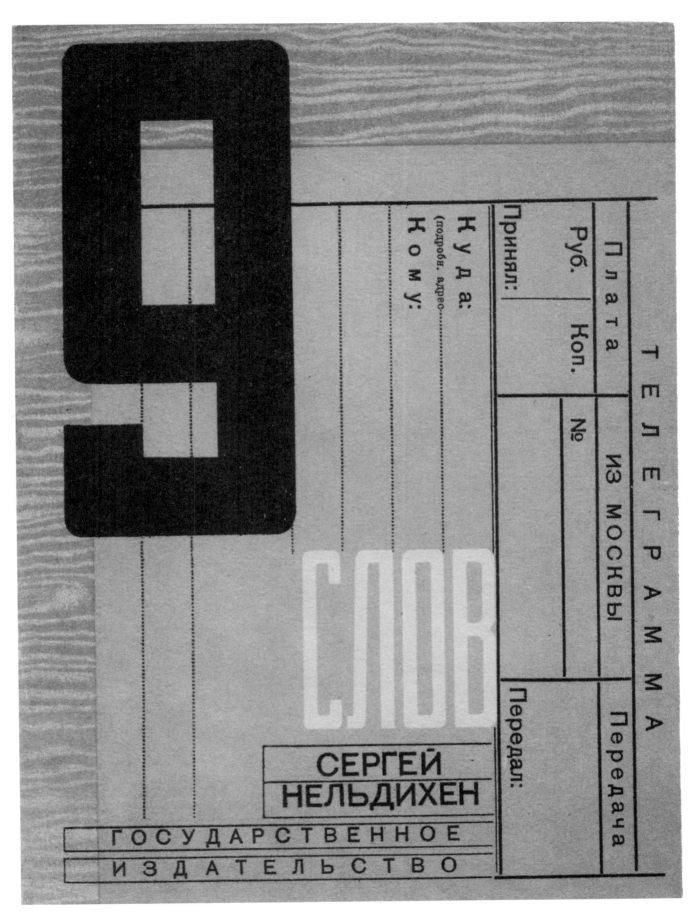

Book cover, *Nine Words*, designed by L. Popova, USSR, 1929

Back cover, *Nine Words* designed by L. Popova, USSR, 1929

Cyrillic alphabet designed by Cehonin, USSR, 1925

АБВГДЕ

ЖЗИКЛМ

НОПРСТ

УФХЦЧЩ

ЪЫЗЮЯ

Stencil alphabet, Russia, c.1920

14

From *The First Counting Book* by F. N. Blekher, Russia, 1934. Courtesy Sasha Lurye collection

Book cover, *The Obesity of Roses (On the Poems of Terentyev and Others)*, illustrated by Aleksei Kruchenykh, Russia, c.1918

КЛАСИЦИСТИЧНА АНТИКВА

А Б В Г Д Е

Ж З И Й К Л М

Н О П Р С Т У

Ф Х Ц Ч Ш Щ

Ъ Ь Ю Я

1 2 3 4 5 6 7 8 9 0

Russian alphabet based on *Bodoni*, USSR, c.1890

From a teaching manual for the study of cyrillic lettering, USSR, c.1940. Courtesy Verlag Hermann Schmidt, Mainz

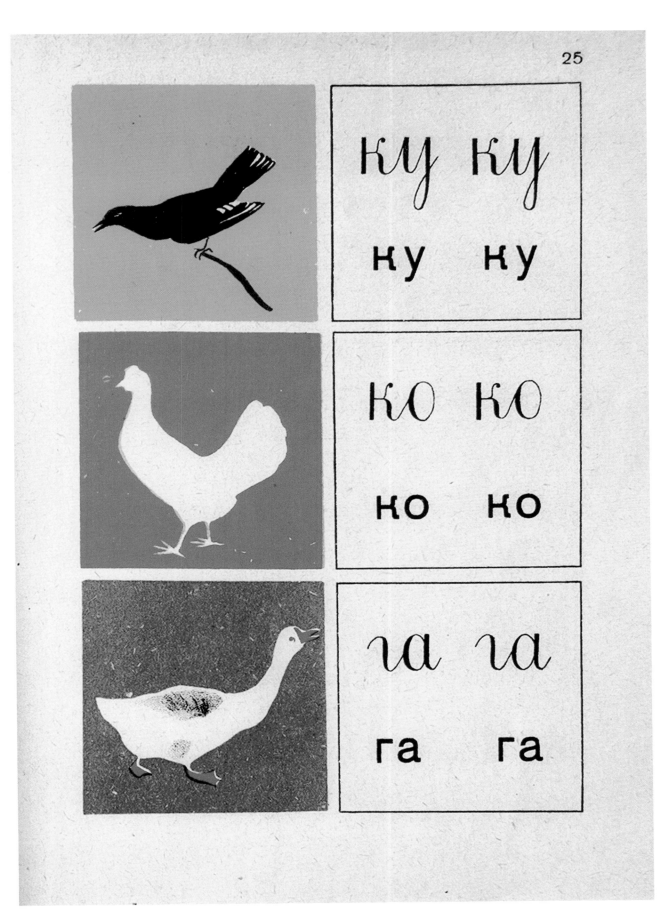

From *A Sparkle, An Easy ABC* by M. Teryaeva, USSR, 1930. Courtesy Sasha Lurye collection

Nautical alphabet from a board game, Russia, c.1910

Back cover of *Wonder Things*, designed by Boris Pokrovsky, USSR, 1928. Courtesy Sasha Lurye collection

СЕМАФОРНАЯ АЗБУКА

Semaphore flag symbols, USSR, c.1952

Front and back cover of school kit, USSR, 1968. Courtesy Pollocks Toy Museum

ТЕТРАДЬ

АЗБУКА

ММП РСФСР
УМП Исполкома Ленгорсовета
Полиграфическая ф-ка № 1
г. Ленинград, Прилукская, 21.
По заказу Лен. базы Роскультторга
Зак. № 1002 Тир. 200000 1968 года

Illustrations for *Coloring Book* by Nikolai Troshin, USSR, 1927. Courtesy Sasha Lurye collection

Book cover, *The Blush of Autumn* by G. Rybintsev, designed by N. Krymov, Russia, 1914

Book cover, *The Record Book* by L. Kassil, designed by Kukryniksy, USSR, 1934

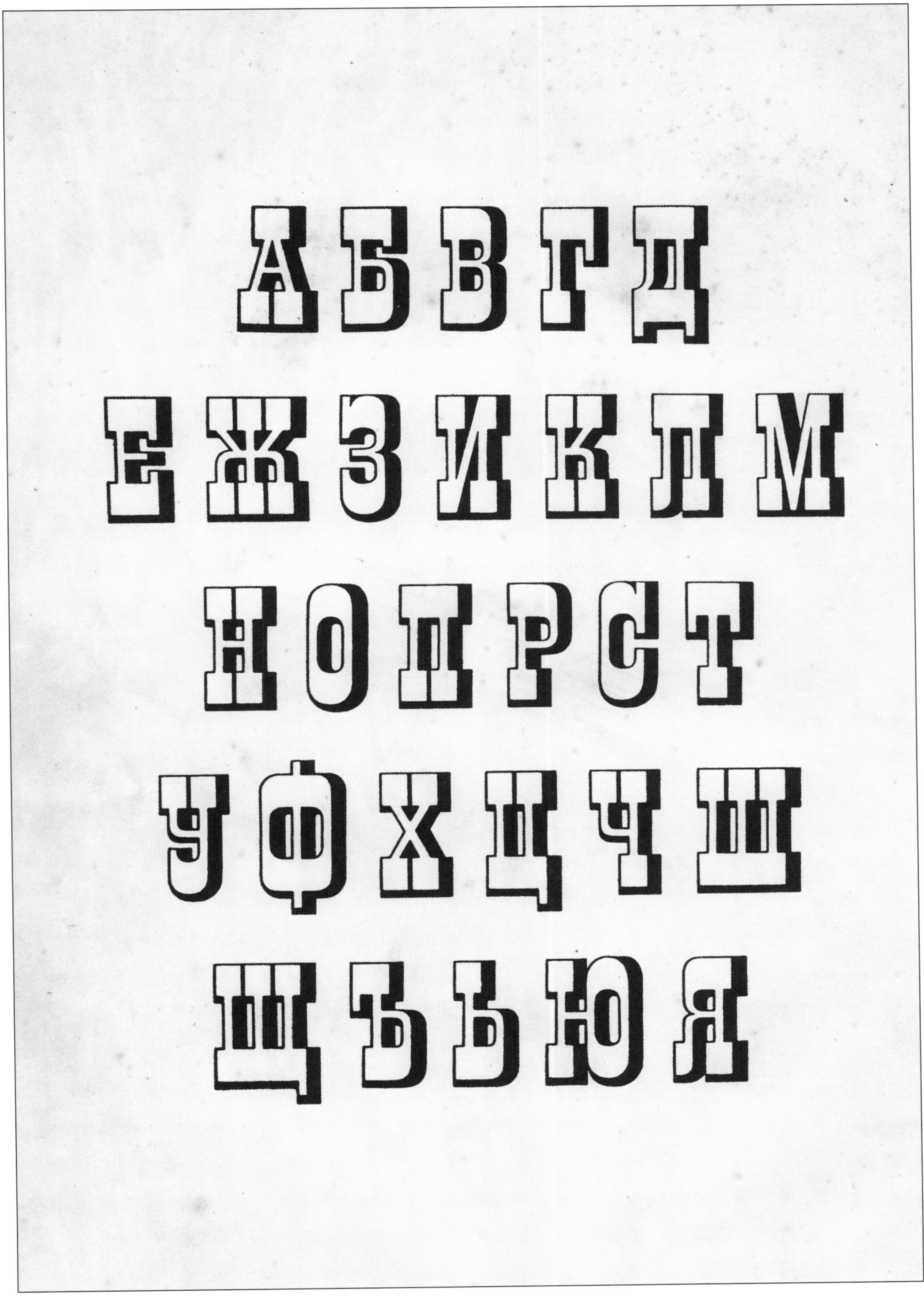

АБВГД
ЕЖЗИКЛМ
НОПРСТ
УФХЦЧШ
ЩЪЬѢЮЯ

Typeface, Russia, c.1905. Courtesy Pentagram

АБВГД
ЕЖЗИК
ЛМНОП
РСТУФХ
ЦЧЩЦЯ
1234567890

Typeface, Russia, c.1905. Courtesy Pentagram

Title page of *Zohna and Brides*, designed by Ilya Zdanevich, USSR, c.1925. Courtesy Misha Anikst

Sheet music cover for *Musicians of the World: Unite!* by Pavel Kuznetsov, USSR, 1925

From the book *Learn Artists*, drawing by A. Kruchenykh, Russia, 1917

From *About This Book* by B. Zhitkov, illustrated by Mikhail Tsekhanovksy, USSR, 1927

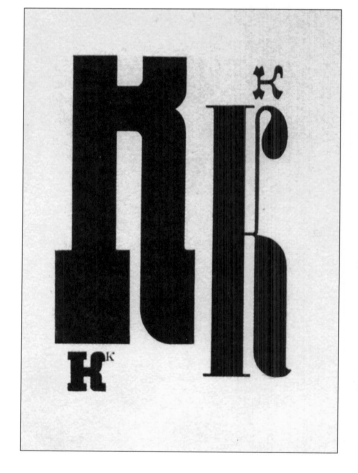

Book cover, *The Rocks* by V. Zybin, Russia, 1914

Front and back cover for *I Am a Printer* by Ekaterina Zonnenstrahl, USSR, 1932. Courtesy Sasha Lurye collection

ТЕКСТ И РИСУНКИ

Е. ЗОННЕНШТРАЛЬ
К. КУЗНЕЦОВ

Сдано в производство 31/XII 1931 г.
Подписано к печати 25/III 1932 г.
Редактор Е. Шабад.
Техн. редактор О. Соловьев.

Уполномоченный Главлита № Б-17055. Издат. № 2828
Д. 52. Заказ № 286. Тир. 50 000.

1-я типо-литография Огиза РСФСР „Образцовая".
Москва, Валовая, 28.

Book cover, *Airships* by S. Vaza, illustrated by Dmitry Bulanov, USSR, 1928. Courtesy Sasha Lurye collection

Book cover, *Trains* by Sergei Vaza, designed by D. Bulanov, USSR, c.1925. Courtesy Sasha Lurye collection

Illustrations from *I Am a Printer* by Ekaterina Zonnenstrahl, USSR, 1932. Courtesy Sasha Lurye collection

ДЕТ ДОМ

СТЕН СТЕН

ГАЗЕТА

БОРЬБА С ВРЕДИТЕЛЯМИ

АБВГДЕЖЗИ
КЛМНОПРС
ТУФХЦЧШЩ
ЪЫЬЬЭЮЯЙ

РУССКАЯ
СОВЕТСКАЯ
КНИГА
и
ГРАВЮРА

Hand-drawn typeface, Russia, c.1910

Magazine cover, *Makovets* (No. 3) by Vladimir Favorsky, USSR, 1923

Poster design for *The Central Red Army Theatre* by Solomon Telingater, USSR, c.1928

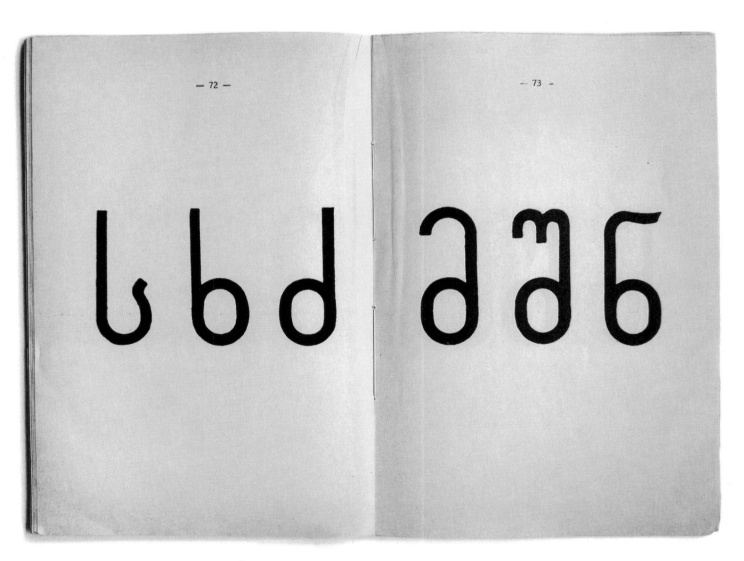

Schoolbook, USSR, date unknown. Courtesy Sasha Lurye collection

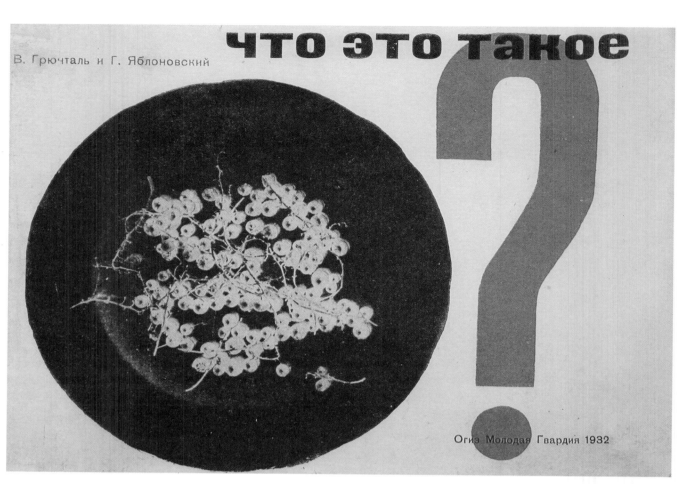

что это такое

В. Грючталь и Г. Яблоновский

?

Огиз Молодая Гвардия 1932

= 56

= 6

Cover and illustration from *What Is This?* by Mikhail Gershenzon, Vladimir Gryuntal, and G. Yablonsky, USSR, 1932. Courtesy Sasha Lurye Collection

Magazine cover, *Divertissements Typographiques*, France c.1935. Courtesy David Batterham

Magazine cover, *Arts et Métiers Graphiques* (No.32), France, 1932

Cover and pages from *Le Témoin*, designed by Paul Iribe, France, 1930s. Courtesy David Batterham

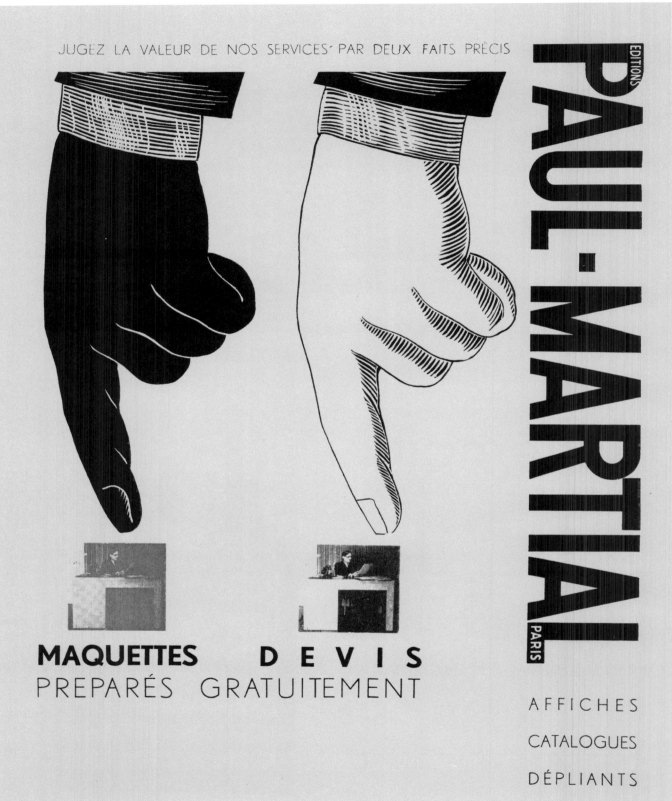

Advertisement from *Arts et Métiers Graphiques*, France, 1930s

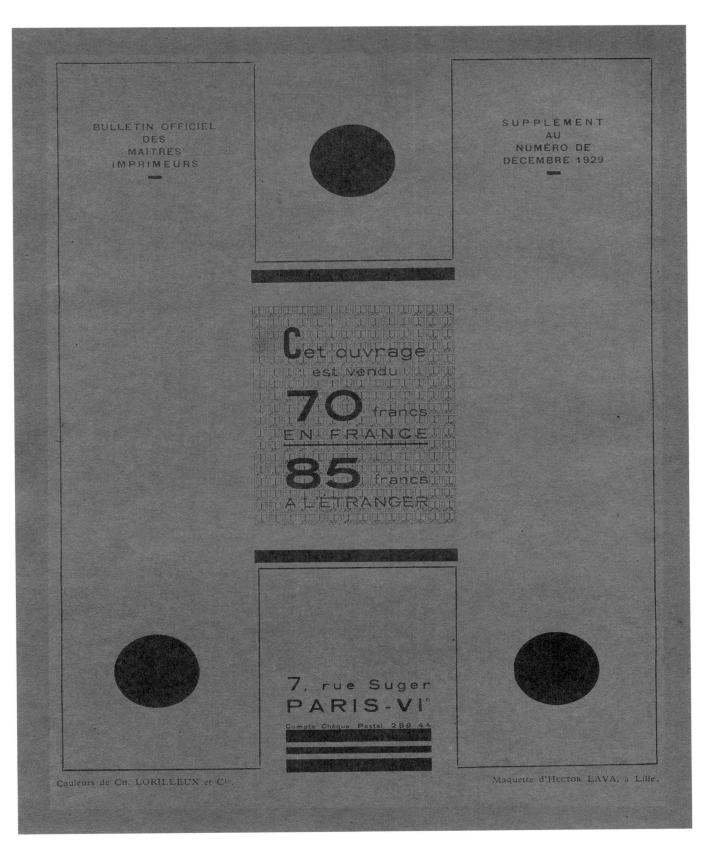

Advertisement from *Arts et Métiers Graphiques*, France, 1930s

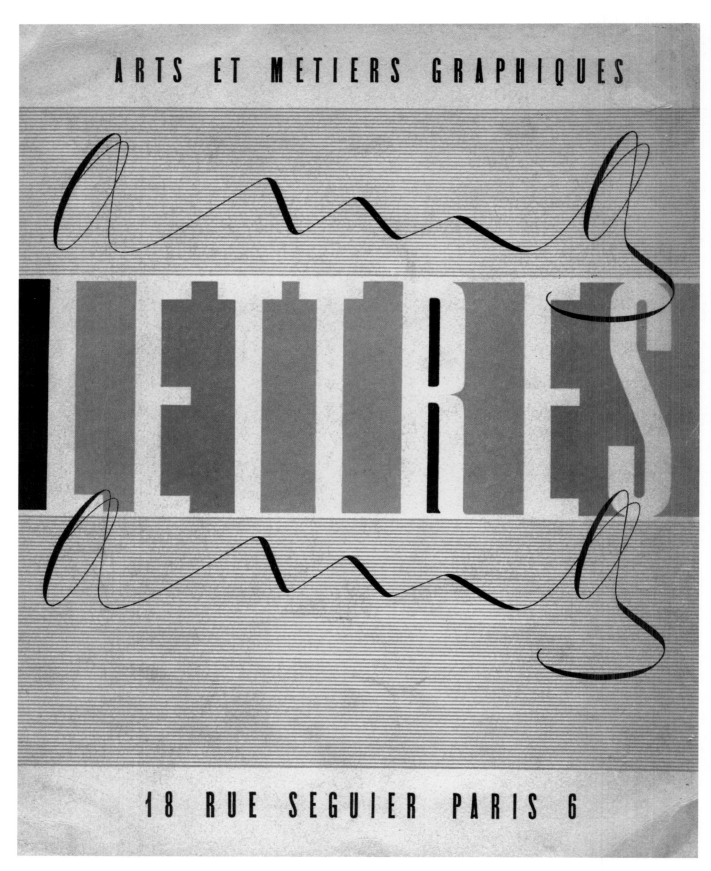

Magazine cover, *Lettres, Arts et Métiers Graphiques*, special edition, France, 1948

ORFÈVRERIE

EL

MEP

MA

BJ

DT

SJ

MODÈLES DE

JEAN PUIFORCAT

BC

SE

AP

103

Page from *Lettres, Arts et Métiers Graphiques*, special edition, France, 1948

ABC OPQ
DEF RST
GHI UVX
JKL WZ
MN -Y-

IMAGES DU MONDE

MER
MARINES MARINS

RACES

PAR
PAUL VALÉRY
de l'Académie Française

PAR
JEAN BRUNHES
de l'Institut

Volumes in-quarto écu de 112 pages, illustrés de 96 planches en héliogravure et brochés dans une couverture illustrée en papier fort. Prix : 30 francs. (On souscrit aux 6 premiers volumes de la collection pour 165 francs, payables : 27 fr. 50 à la réception de chaque volume.)

TOP: Stencil typeface BOTTOM: Advertisement from *Arts et Métiers Graphiques*, France, 1935

From *Arts et Métiers Graphiques*, designed by Roland Ansteau, France, 1930s

Magazine cover, *Arts et Métiers Graphiques*, France, 1930s

Page with a menu from *Arts et Métiers Graphiques*, France, 1930s

ORFÈVRERIE

SC

PQ

AX

FL

FF

MODÈLES DE

GP

JEAN PUIFORCAT

NA

GD

From *Arts et Métiers Graphiques*, special edition, France, 1948

ARTS ET MÉTIERS GRAPHIQUES

AM
G
61

Magazine cover, *Arts et Métiers Graphiques*, France, 1930s

Publicité Dam.

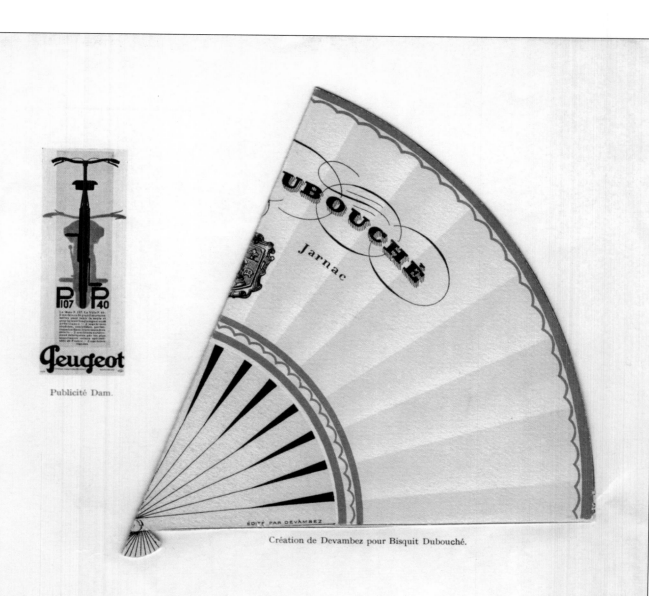

Création de Devambez pour Bisquit Dubouché.

Annonce pour les montres Lip.

Page d'annonce (Édit. Paul-Martial).

Dessin de Francis Bernard
(Édit. Paul-Martial).

From *Arts et Métiers Graphiques*, France, 1930s. Courtesy David Batterham

Advertisement from *Arts et Métiers Graphiques*, France, 1930s

ORFÈVRERIE

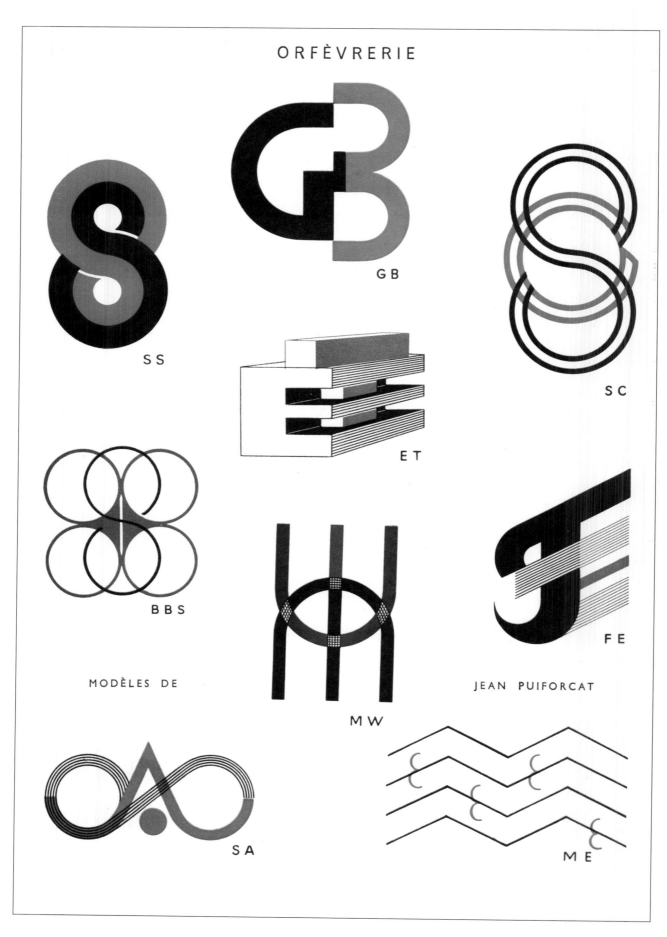

SS

GB

SC

ET

BBS

MW

MODÈLES DE

JEAN PUIFORCAT

FE

SA

ME

From *Arts et Métiers Graphiques*, special edition, France, 1948

Magazine cover, *Le Mot*, designed by Paul Iribe, France, 1914. Courtesy David Batterham

EROTICISM

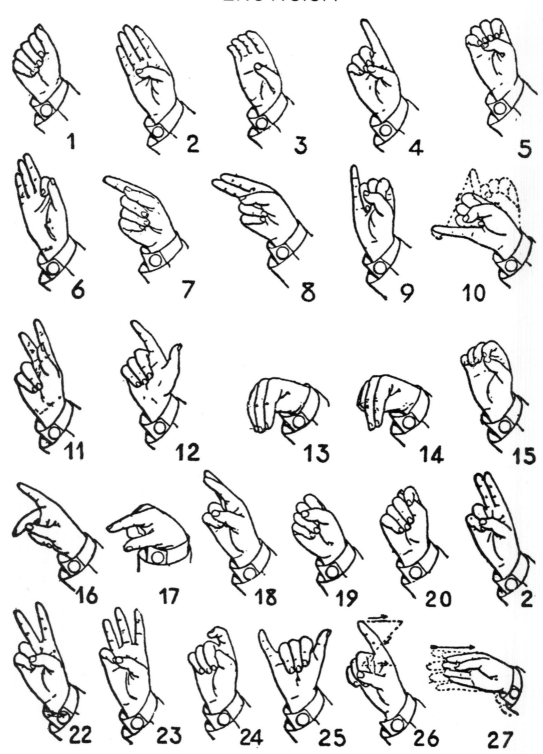

1. Accost 2. Burgle 3. Cunnilungate 4. Deflower 5. Ensnare 6. Fuck 7. Gallivant
8. Harass 9. Irrumate 10. Jismify 11. Kink 12. Lesbianise 13. Masturbate 14. Nidify
15. Occult 16. Pedicate 17. Quench 18. Ream 19. Syphilize 20. Tup 21. Urticate
22. Violate 23. Waggle 24 Xiphoidify 25. Yonirise 26. Zoogonise 27. Recommence

A surrealist provocation: page from the *Da Costa Encyclopedia*, anonymously and collectively edited, France, 1947

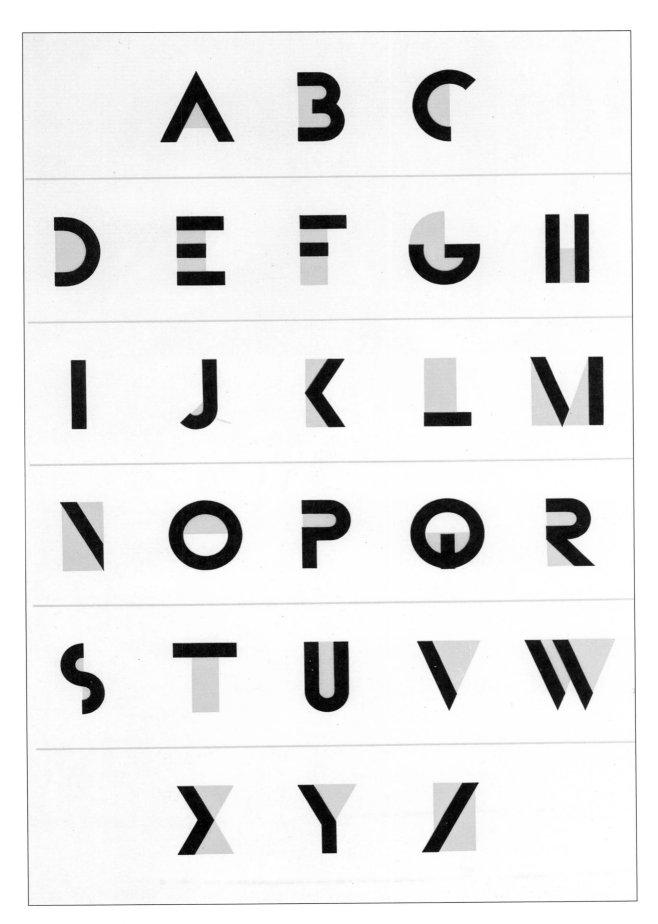

Alphabet, Bifur by A. M. Cassandre, France, 1929. Courtesy Klingspoor Museum, Offenbach

From *First Book of Images: Children's Everyday Objects*, by Emmanuel Souget, France, 1932

From *A Photographic Alphabet* by Pauline David, designed by Gaston Karquel, France, date unknown

Lettres majuscules.

ABCDE
FGHIJK
LMNOP
QRSTU
VWXYZ

From *Buffon Alphabet des Oiseaux*, France, 1890. Courtesy Pentagram

PABLO PICASSO

Voyez ce peintre il prend les choses avec leur ombre aussi et d'un coup d'œil sublimatoire
Il se déchire en accords profonds et agréables à respirer tel l'orgue que j'aime entendre
Des Arlequines jouent dans le rose et bleus d'un beau-ciel   Ce souvenir revit
les rêves   et les actives mains   Orient plein de glaciers   L'hiver est rigoureux
Lustres   or toile irisée or   loi des stries de feu   fond en murmurant.
Bleu   flamme légère   argent des ondes   bleues après le grand cri
Tout   en restant   elles touchent   cette sirène violon
Faons   lourdes ailes   l'incandesce   quelques brasses encore
Bourdons   femmes striées   éclat de   plongeon-diamant
Arlequins   semblables à Dieu   en variété   Aussi distingués qu'un lac
Fleurs   brillant comme deux   perles   monstres qui palpitent
Lys   cerclés d'or,   je n'étais pas seul!   fais onduler les remords
Nouveau monde très matinal   montant de l'énorme mer
L'aventure de ce vieux cheval   en Amérique
Au soir de la pêche merveilleuse   l'œil du masque
Air de petits violons au fond des   anges rangés
Dans le couchant puis au bout de   l'an des dieux
Regarde la tête géante et immense   la main verte
L'argent sera vite remplacé par   tout notre or
Morte pendue à l'hameçon... c'est   la danse bleue
L'humide voix des acrobates   des maisons
Grimace parmi les assauts du vent   qui s'assoupit
Ouis les vagues et le fracas d'une   femme bleue
Enfin la grotte à l'atmosphère dorée   par la vertu
Ce saphir veiné   il faut rire!
Rois de phosphore   sous les arbres les bottines entre des plumes bleues
La danse des   dix mouches   lui fait face quand il songe à toi
Le cadre bleu   tandis que   l'air agile s'ouvrait aussi
  Au milieu des   regrets dans une vaste grotte.
Prends les araignées roses   à la nage
Regrets d'invisibles pièges   l'air
Paisible se souleva mais sur le clavier   musiques
Guitare-tempête   ô gai trémolo
O gai trémolo   ô gai trémolo
Il ne rit pas   l'artiste-peintre
Ton pauvre   étincellement pâle
L'ombre agile   d'un soir d'été qui meurt
Immense désir   et l'aube émerge des eaux si lumineuses
Je vis nos yeux   diamants enfermer le reflet du ciel vert et
J'entendis sa voix   qui dorait les forêts tandis que vous pleuriez
L'acrobate à cheval le poète à moustaches un oiseau mort et tant d'enfants sans larmes
Choses cassées des livres déchirés des couches de poussière et des aurores déferlant!

GUILLAUME APOLLINAIRE

Calligramme by Guillaume Apollinaire, France, 1917

Book cover, *The Chapel at Ronchamp*, designed by Le Corbusier, UK, 1957

Magazine cover, *L'oeil*, France, 1955

216

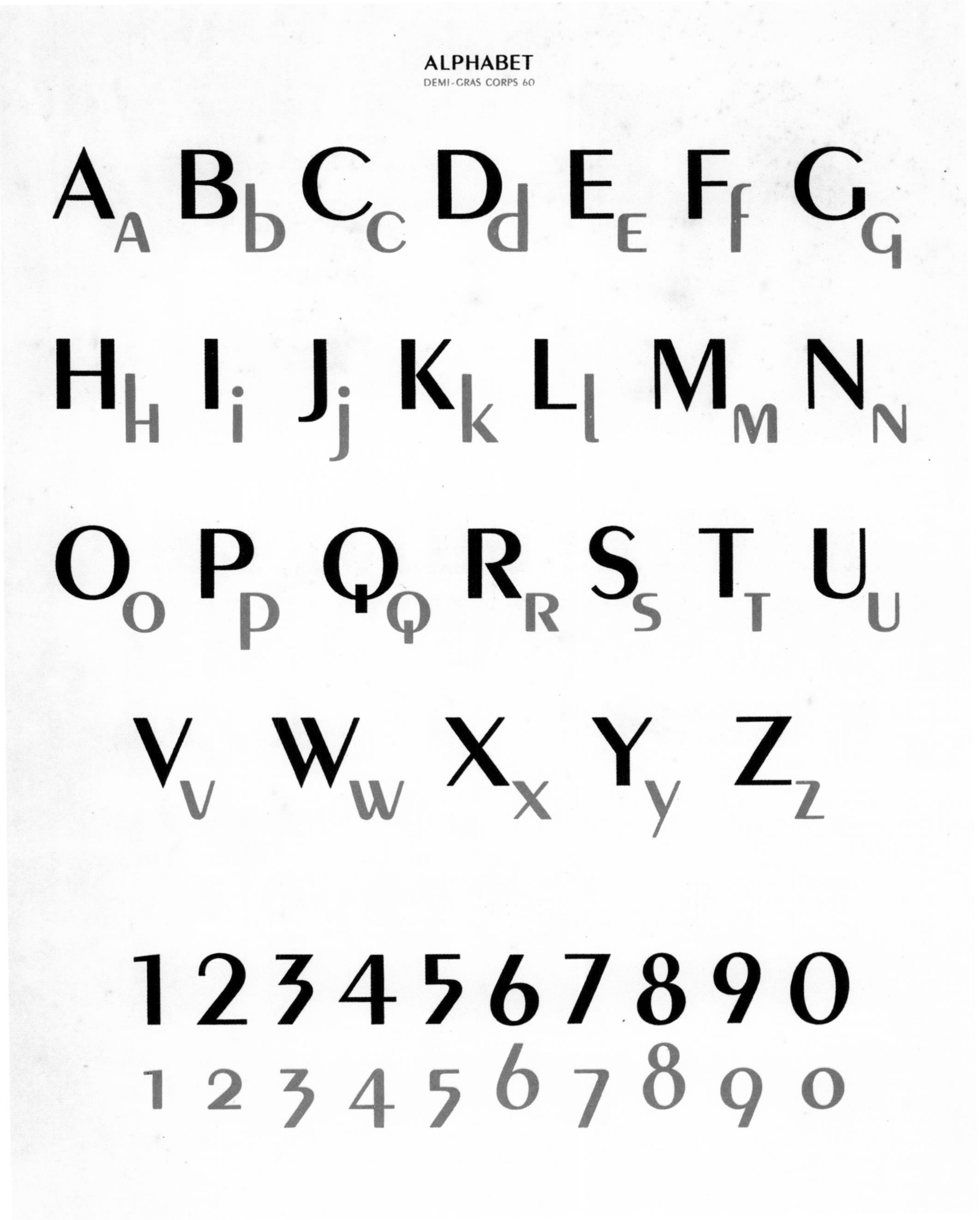

A A B b C c D d E e F f G g

H h I i J j K k L l M m N n

O o P p Q q R r S s T t U u

V v W w X x Y y Z z

1 2 3 4 5 6 7 8 9 0
1 2 3 4 5 6 7 8 9 0

Peignot typeface designed by A. M. Cassandre, France, 1937

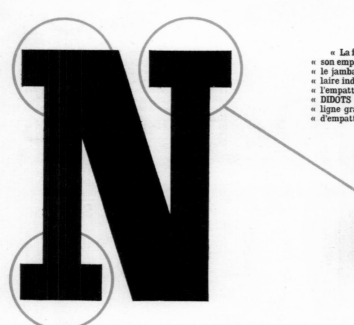

« La famille d'un caractère se détermine d'après
« son empattement, c'est-à-dire le trait qui termine
« le jambage des capitales. L'empattement triangu-
« laire indique la famille des ELZÉVIRS ou ANCIENS,
« l'empattement rectiligne maigre, la famille des
« DIDOTS ou CLASSIQUES, l'empattement recti-
« ligne gras la famille des EGYPTIENNES, l'absence
« d'empattement la famille des ANTIQUES ».

EMPATTEMENT
RECTILIGNE
G R A S

ABCDEFGHIJKLM
NOPQRSTUVWXYZ

abcdefghijklm
nopqrstuvwxyz
1234567890

TYPE D'EGYPTIENNE : LA COMPACTE

L'ART DE RECONNAITRE UN CARACTÈRE
(PRINCIPE DE THIBAUDEAU)

Egyptian typeface reproduced in *Arts et Métiers Graphiques*, France, 1934

Cover of *d'Art Moderne*, France, 1932. Courtesy Alan Fletcher

ABCDE
FGHIJK
LMNOPQ
RSTUV
WXYZ

Didot typeface, France, c.1810

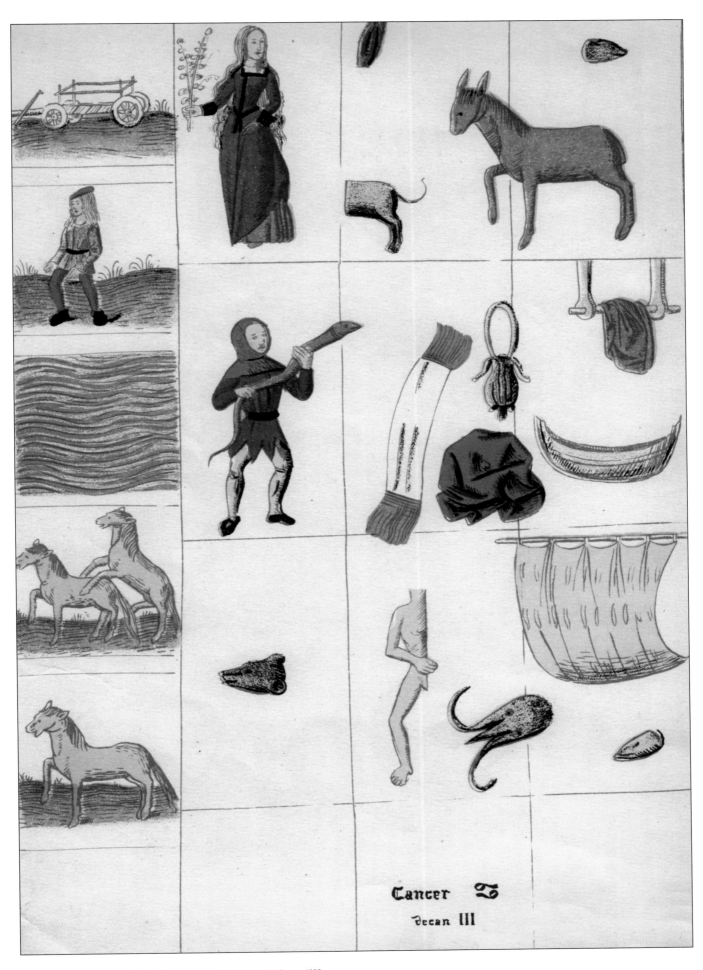

Medieval horoscope from the article "Les Douze Maisons du Ciel" from *Verve*, France, 1938

Poster for Florent pastilles designed by A. M. Cassandre, France, 1930s

CHAMBORD MAIGRE

ABCDEFGHIJK
LMNOPQR
STUVWXYZ

ÇÆŒÉÈËÊ&-?!()«»'´;,.

abcdefghijklmn
opqrstuvwxyz

çæœàäâéèëêïîöôùüû

1 2 3 4 5 6 7 8 9 0

Chambord Maigre, from a typefounders' manual, France, c.1940. Courtesy Verlag Hermann Schmidt, Mainz

ÉDITION IN ENGLISH

CHRISTMAS 1938

Back cover of *XXth Century* (English edition), France, 1938. Courtesy Brian Webb collection

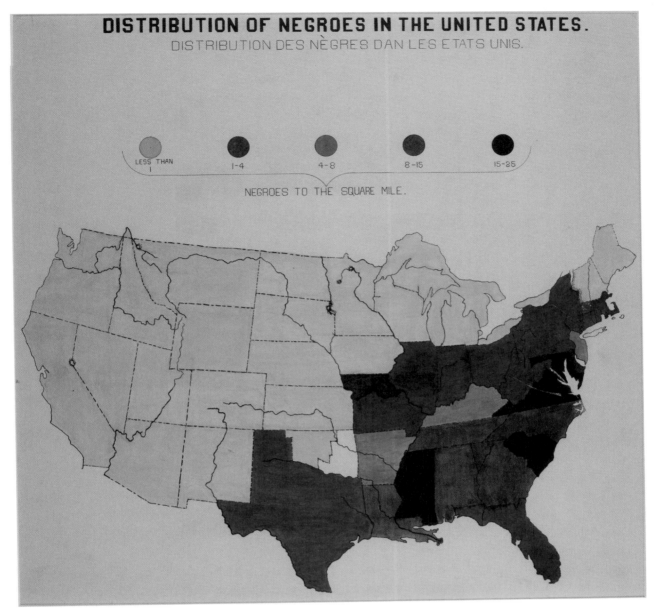

DISTRIBUTION OF NEGROES IN THE UNITED STATES.
DISTRIBUTION DES NÈGRES DAN LES ETATS UNIS.

LESS THAN 1   1–4   4–8   8–15   15–25

NEGROES TO THE SQUARE MILE.

Statistical chart by W. E. B. Du Bois: *Distribution of Negroes in the United States*, USA, c.1900

W. E. B. DU BOIS: THE LIVES OF AFRICAN-AMERICANS AT THE TURN OF THE CENTURY

At the 1900 Paris Exposition Universelle—the stupendous world's fair celebrating the achievements of the nineteenth century and the glorious prospects for the twentieth—the distinguished African-American sociologist and activist W. E. B. Du Bois devised a brilliant exhibit intended to show (in his words) "the history of the American Negro, his present condition, his education and his literature." Among much other compelling documentation (photographs, books, and other materials) Du Bois presented a spectacular display of hand-drawn and colored statistical charts, maps, and diagrams. During his time teaching economics, history and sociology at Atlanta University, Du Bois and his students, especially William Andrew Rogers, prepared the infographics. The clarity and diversity of the charts and graphs demonstrate an extraordinary mastery of what became known much later in the new century as *information graphics*. "The need of the South is knowledge and culture," wrote Du Bois in his 1903 classic, *The Souls of Black Folk*. How to express this need better than in these beautiful graphics that convey socioeconomic knowledge and reveal cultural truth?

OCCUPATIONS OF NEGROES AND WHITES IN GEORGIA.

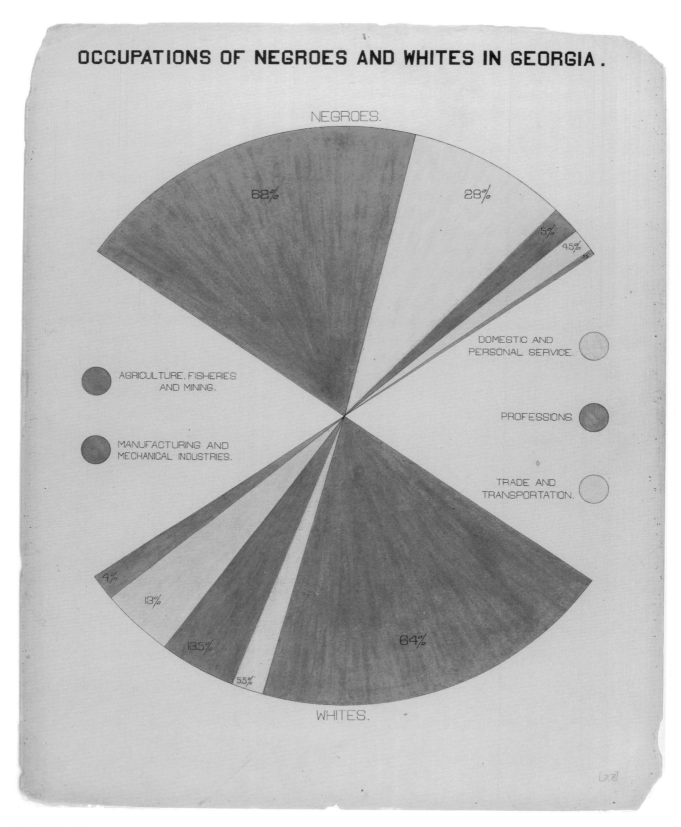

NEGROES.

62%

28%

5%

4.5%

DOMESTIC AND
PERSONAL SERVICE.

AGRICULTURE, FISHERIES
AND MINING.

PROFESSIONS.

MANUFACTURING AND
MECHANICAL INDUSTRIES.

TRADE AND
TRANSPORTATION.

4%

13%

13.5%

5.5%

64%

WHITES.

Statistical chart by W. E. B. Du Bois, *Occupations of Negroes and Whites in Georgia*, USA, c.1900

228

Religion of American Negroes.

Religion des Nègres Americains.

Done by Atlanta University.

Catholics	14,517.
Protestants	2,659,460.
Protestant Sects:	
Baptists	
Methodists	
Presbyterians	
Congregationalists	
Miscellaneous	

Statistical chart by W. E. B. Du Bois, *Religion of American Negroes*, USA, c.1900

American Negro newspapers and periodicals.

Journaux et publications periodiques Nègres aux Etats Unis.

Done by Atlanta University.

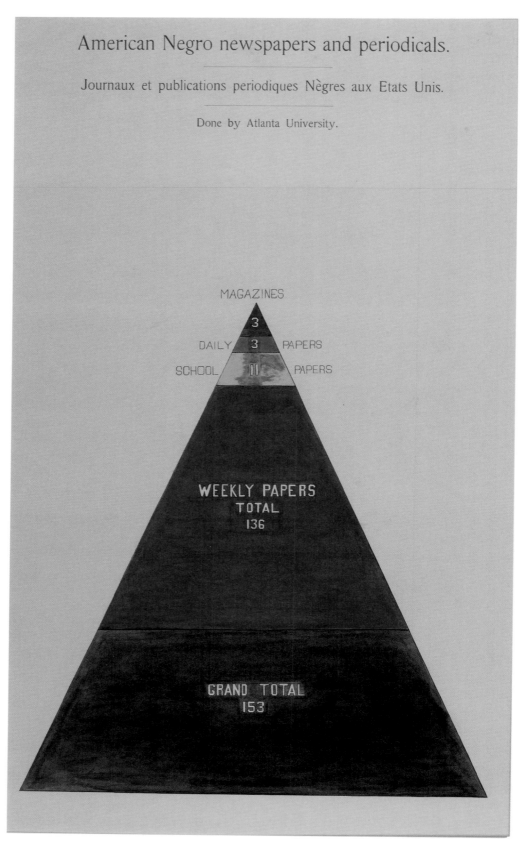

Statistical chart by W. E. B. Du Bois, *Negro Population of Georgia by Counties*, USA, c.1900

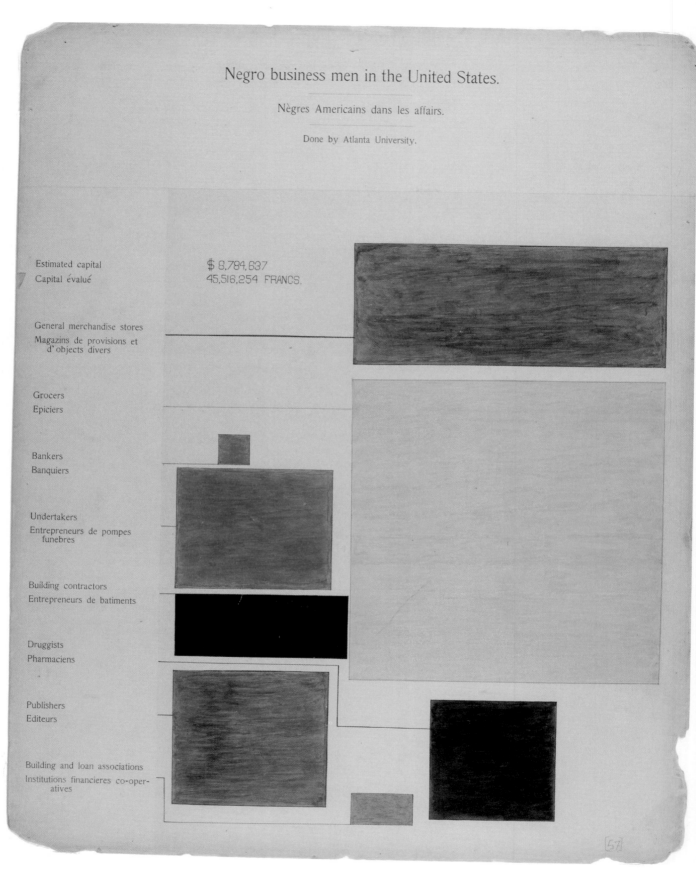

Negro business men in the United States.

Nègres Americains dans les affaires.

Done by Atlanta University.

Estimated capital / Capital évalué — $ 8,784,637 / 45,516,254 FRANCS.

General merchandise stores / Magazins de provisions et d'objects divers

Grocers / Epiciers

Bankers / Banquiers

Undertakers / Entrepreneurs de pompes funebres

Building contractors / Entrepreneurs de batiments

Druggists / Pharmaciens

Publishers / Editeurs

Building and loan associations / Institutions financieres co-operatives

Statistical chart by W. E. B. Du Bois, *Negro Business Men in the United States*, USA, c.1900

CITY AND RURAL POPULATION.
1890.

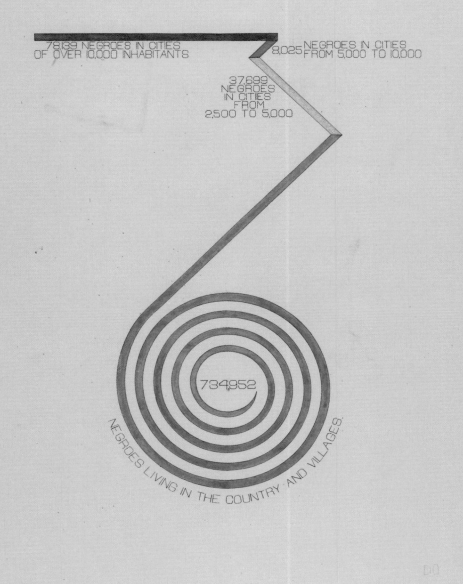

78,139 NEGROES IN CITIES OF OVER 10,000 INHABITANTS

8,025 NEGROES IN CITIES FROM 5,000 TO 10,000

37,699 NEGROES IN CITIES FROM 2,500 TO 5,000

734,952

NEGROES LIVING IN THE COUNTRY AND VILLAGES.

Statistical chart by W. E. B. Du Bois, *City and Rural Population 1890*, USA, c.1900

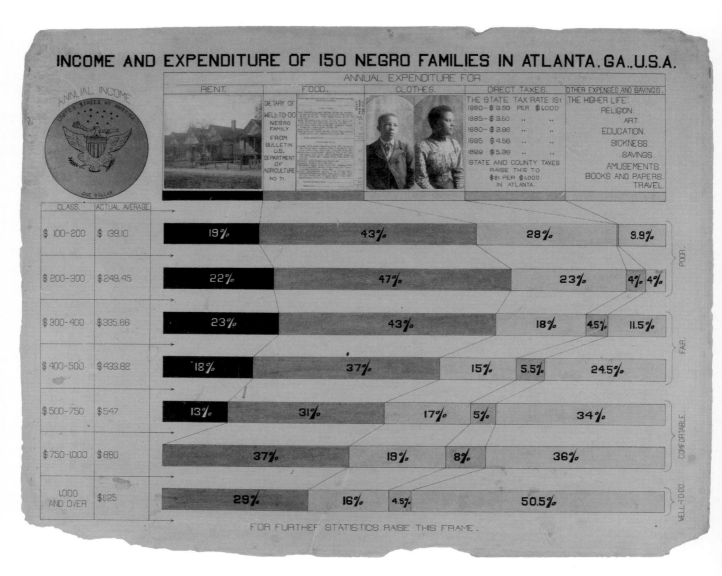

Statistical chart by W. E. B. Du Bois, *Income and Expenditure of 150 Negro Families in Atlanta*, USA, c.1900

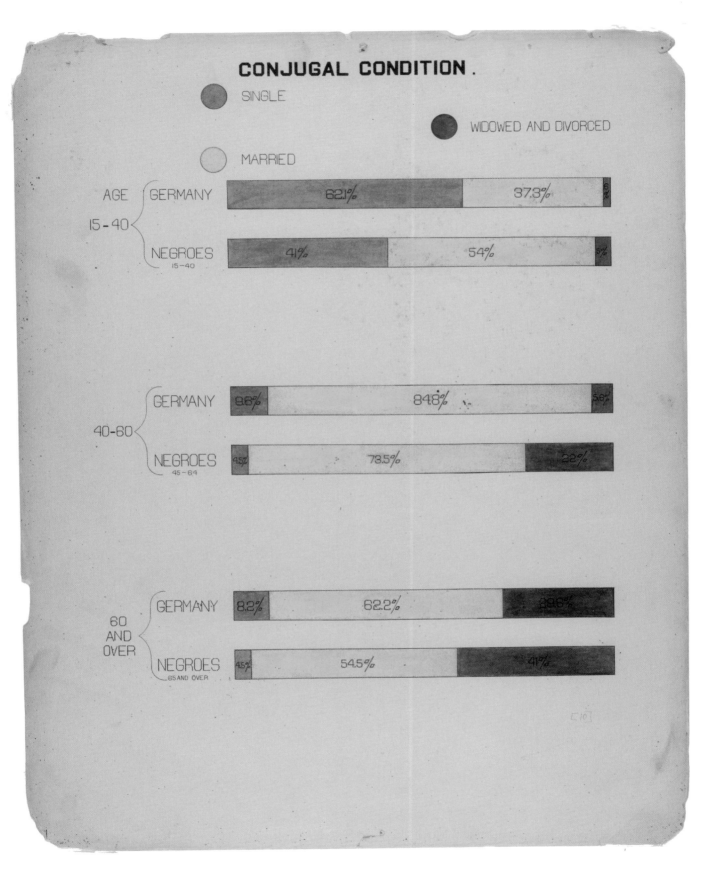

CONJUGAL CONDITION.

Statistical chart by W. E. B. Du Bois, *Conjugal Condition*, USA, c.1900

235

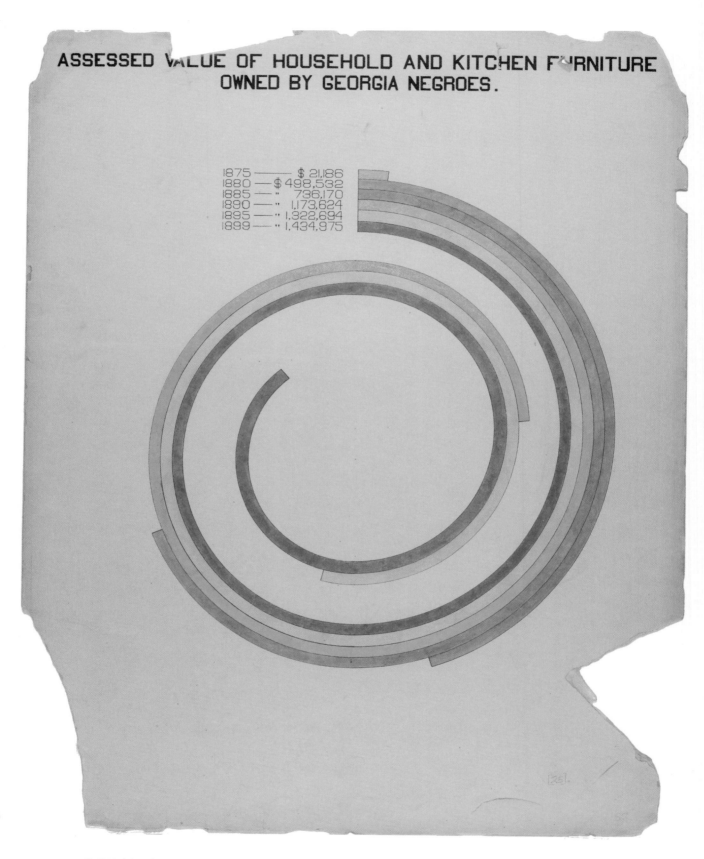

ASSESSED VALUE OF HOUSEHOLD AND KITCHEN FURNITURE OWNED BY GEORGIA NEGROES.

1875	——	$ 21,186
1880	— $	498,532
1885	— ''	736,170
1890	— ''	1,173,624
1895	— ''	1,322,694
1899	— ''	1,434,975

Statistical chart by W. E. B. Du Bois, *Assessed Valuation of All Taxable Property Owned by Georgia Negroes*, USA, c.1900

Statistical chart by W. E. B. Du Bois, *Proportion of Freemen and Slaves Among American Negroes*, USA, c.1900

Crime among American Negroes.

Criminalité parmi les Nègres Americains.

Done by Atlanta University.

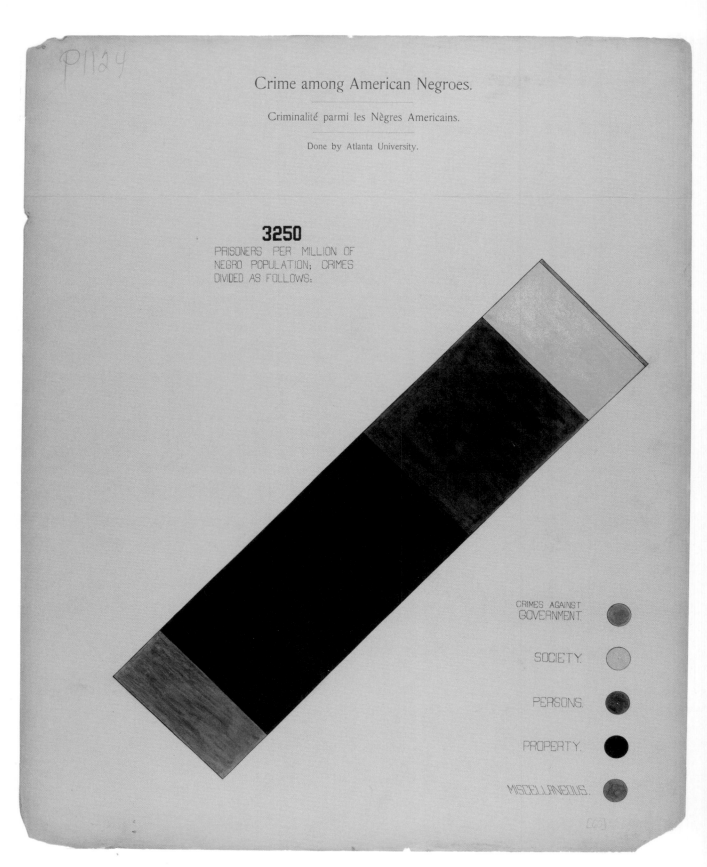

3250
PRISONERS PER MILLION OF
NEGRO POPULATION; CRIMES
DIVIDED AS FOLLOWS:

CRIMES AGAINST
GOVERNMENT.

SOCIETY.

PERSONS.

PROPERTY.

MISCELLANEOUS.

Statistical chart by W. E. B. Du Bois, *Crime Among American Negroes*, USA, c.1900

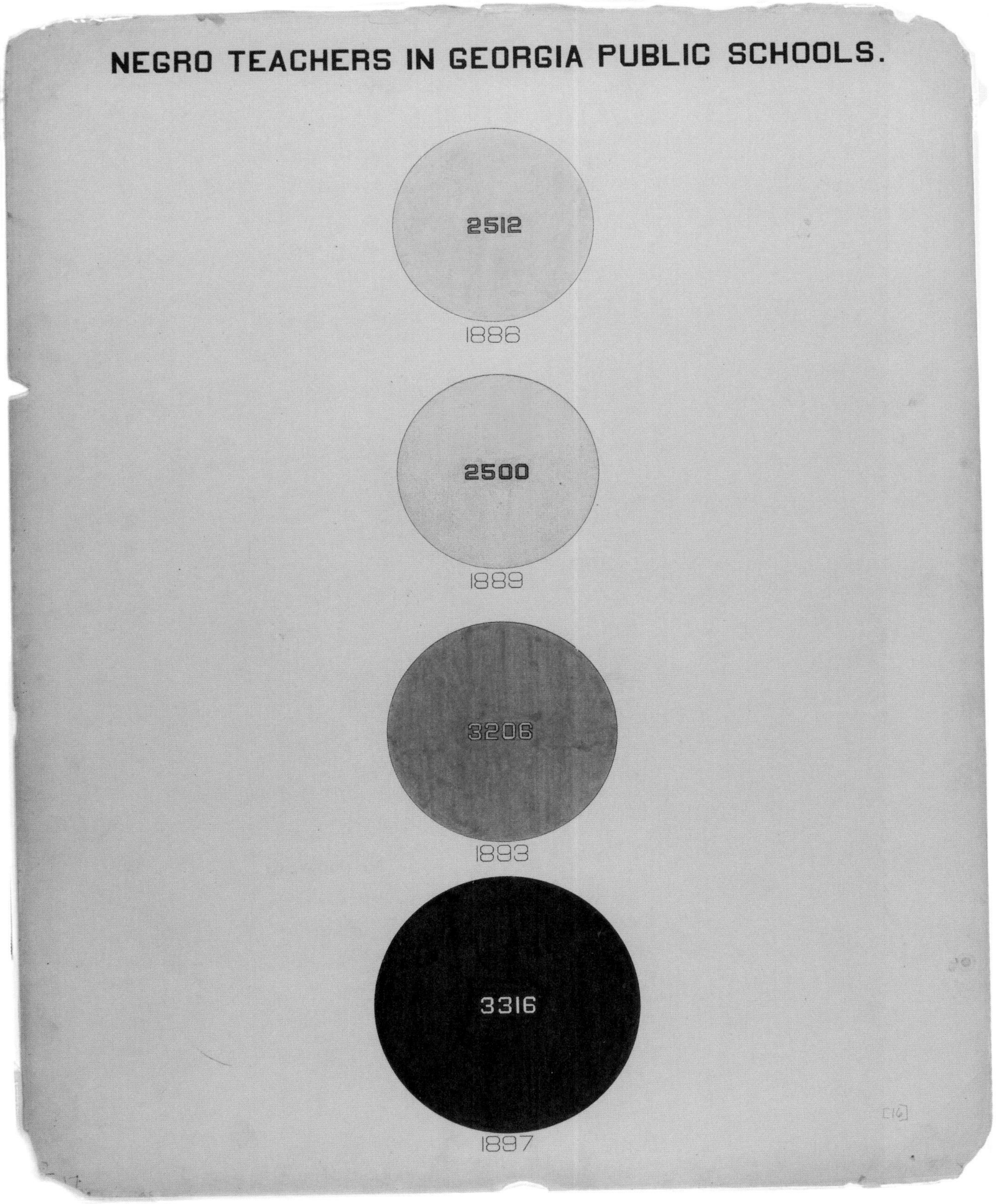

NEGRO TEACHERS IN GEORGIA PUBLIC SCHOOLS.

2512

1886

2500

1889

3206

1893

3316

1897

Statistical chart by W. E. B. Du Bois, *Negro Teachers in Georgia Public Schools*, USA, c.1900

ASSESSED VALUATION OF ALL TAXABLE PROPERTY OWNED BY GEORGIA NEGROES.

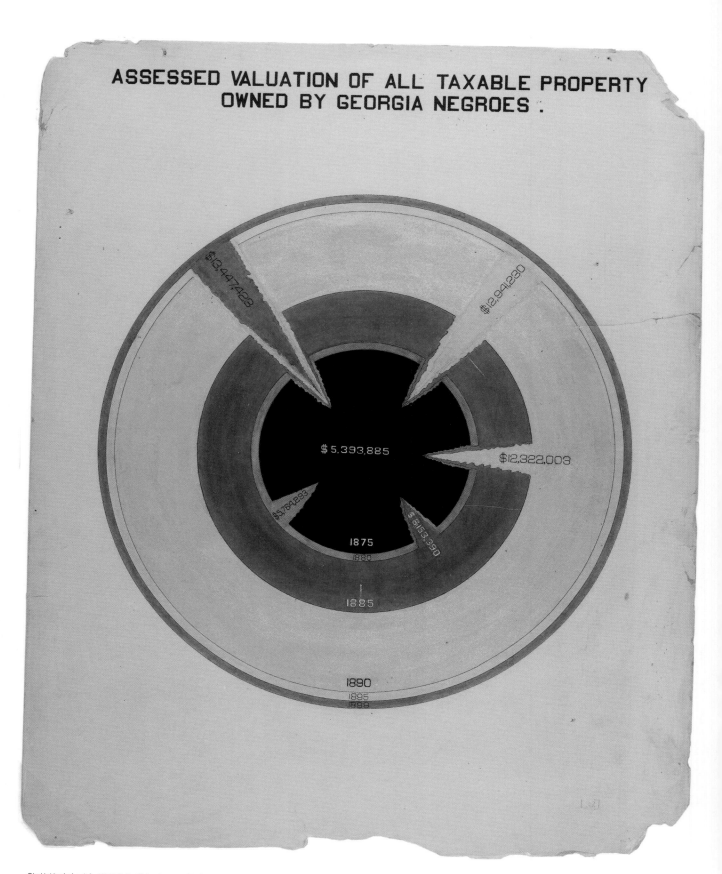

Statistical chart by W. E. B. Du Bois, *Assessed Valuation of All Taxable Property Owned by Georgia Negroes*, USA c.1900

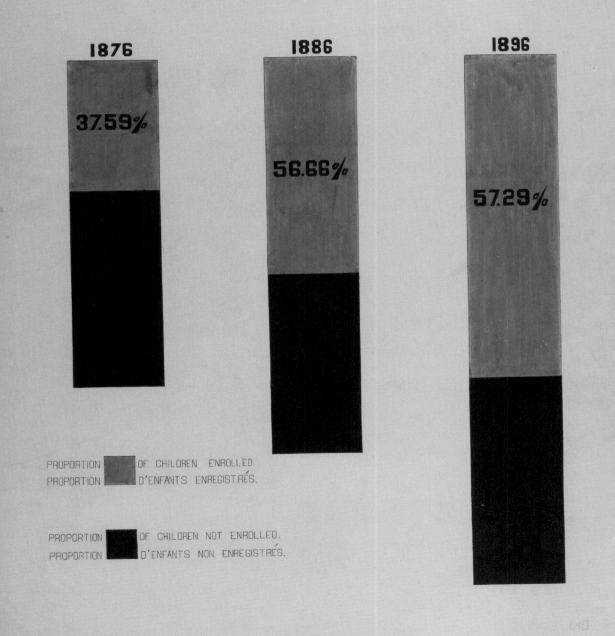

Statistical chart by W. E. B. Du Bois, *Proportion of Total Negro Children of School Age Who Are Enrolled in the Public Schools*, USA, c.1900

Occupations in which American Negroes are engaged.

Occupations et industries des Nègres Americains.

Done by Atlanta University.

BOTH SEXES.
HOMMES ET FEMMES.

MALES.
HOMMES.

FEMALES.
FEMMES.

AGRICULTURE MINING AND FISHING.

PROFESSIONS.

DOMESTIC AND PERSONAL SERVICE.

COMMERCE AND TRANSPORTATION. MANUFACTURING AND MECHANICAL INDUSTRIES.

AGRICULTURE, PÊCHE ET MINES.

PROFESSIONS.

SERVICE DOMESTIQUE ET PERSONNEL.

COMMERCE ET TRANSPORT, INDUSTRIES MANUFACTURIERES ET MÉCANIQUES.

Statistical chart by W. E. B. Du Bois, *Occupations in Which American Negroes Are Engaged*, USA, c.1900

Poster for Borsalino hats designed by Max Huber, Italy, c.1950

Book cover, *Futurism* by F. T. Marinetti, Italy, 1920

Book cover, *First Italian Aerial Dictionary* by F. T. Marinetti, designed by Fedele Azari, Italy, 1929

Magazine cover, *Campo Grafico*, Italian Futurism issue designed by Bona, Italy, 1939

TRIESTE

MADERA

From *Tabacchi Italiani Catalogo* (Italian State Monopoly), Italy, 1930. Courtesy David Batterham

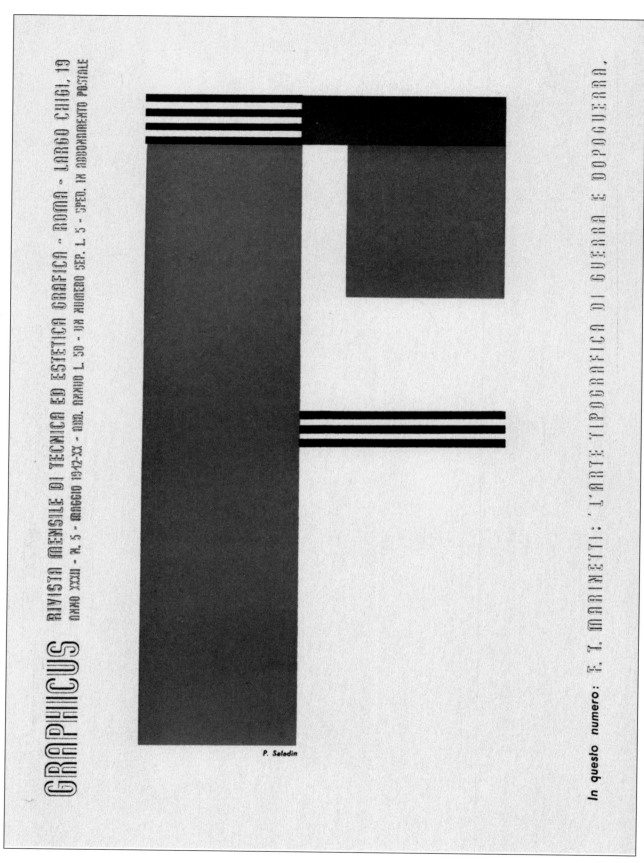

GRAPHICUS RIVISTA MENSILE DI TECNICA ED ESTETICA GRAFICA - ROMA - LARGO CHIGI, 19
ANNO XXII - N. 5 - MAGGIO 1942-XX - ABB. ANNUO L. 50 - UN NUMERO SEP. L. 5 - SPED. IN ABBONAMENTO POSTALE

P. Saladin

In questo numero: F. T. MARINETTI: 'L'ARTE TIPOGRAFICA DI GUERRA E DOPOGUERRA',

Magazine cover, *Campo Grafico*, Italian Futurism issue designed by P. Saladin, Italy, 1942

248

Book cover for *Preserved Love* by F. T. Marinetti, designed by Carlo Petrucci, illustration by Pannaggi, Italy, 1927

LE RELIGIONI NEL MONDO
(1936)

CRISTIANI — MAOMETTANI — CULTI PRIMIT. — INDUISTI — BUDDISTI CONFU-CIANISTI E SCINTOISTI — ATEI

BIANCHI — NEGRI — INDO-ATLANTICI — GIALLI

OGNI FIGURA: CENTO MILIONI DI UOMINI

Tav. 190

Statistics chart, *Religions of the World*, from *The Bompiani Practical Encyclopedia, Volume 1: Culture*, Italy, 1938

Fregio Mecano, typeface from a typefounders' catalogue, Italy, c.1930. Courtesy Pentagram. See also page 252

From *Tabacchi Italiani Catalogo* (Italian State Monopoly), Italy, 1930. Courtesy David Batterham

From *Tabacchi Italiani Catalogo* (Italian State Monopoly), Italy, 1930. Courtesy David Batterham

ARAGÓN

ABCDEFGHI
JKLMNÑOPQ
ASTUVWXYZ
Æ.,;:Œ

Aragón, typeface designed by Enric Crous-Vidal, Spain, 1950s. Courtesy Fundación Tipográfica Bauer, Barcelona

Within the specimen:

Crous-Vidal, dont l'exposition à la Galerie d'Orsay fut le "clou" graphique de la rentrée 52, a dédié à Jean Giono et à l'école de Lure ce flamboyant caractère d'inspiration méditerranénne : LES CATALANES

LES CATALANES

Les Catalanes, typeface designed by Enric Crous-Vidal from *Caractère Noël*, Spain, 1952. Courtesy Fundación Tipográfica Bauer, Spain

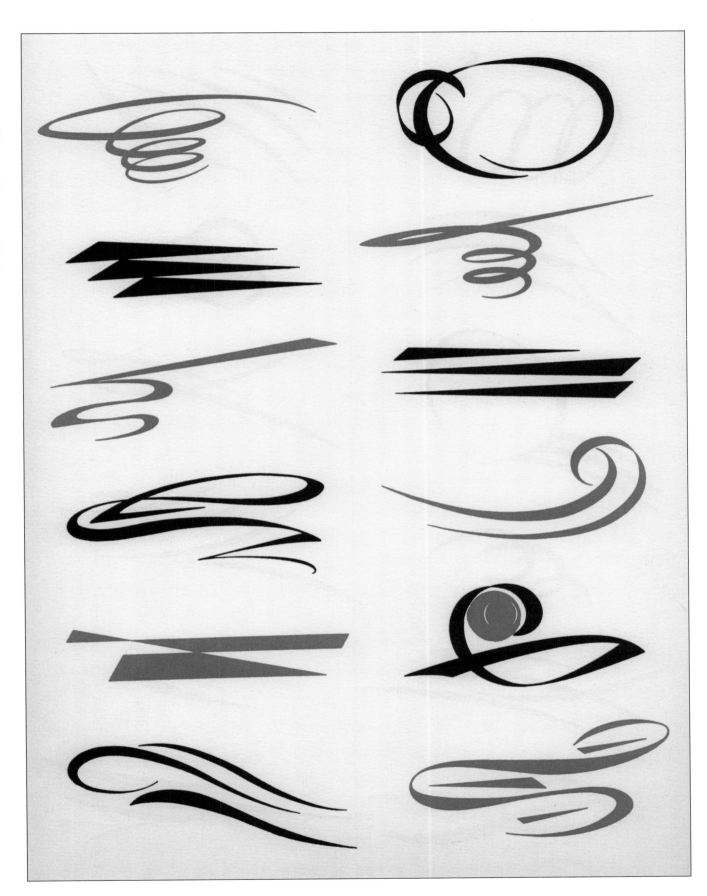

Flourishes designed by Enric Crous-Vidal, Spain, 1953. Courtesy Fundación Tipográfica Bauer, Barcelona

Magazine cover for the literary journal *Ultra*, (No.22), pochoir by the Polish artist Wladyslaw Jahl, Spain, 1921

Pages 261–266 from *Cartilla Escolar Antifascista*, Spain, 1937

THE ANTI-FASCIST SCHOOLBOOK

In 1937 the Second Spanish Republic was deeply embroiled in the savage Civil War against the authoritarian rebellion led by General Francisco Franco. Under the leadership of the Minister of Education, Jesús Hernández Tomás, the Ministry of Public Information issued *Cartilla Escolar Antifascista*, a literacy primer, as an aid to the campaign of the "cultural militias" against illiteracy. The booklet, beautifully designed by Mauricio Amster Cats, who also created the poster advertising the "schoolbook," combined phonetics with politics, identifying the military struggle against authoritarianism with the cultural fight against ignorance. The Spanish Civil War ended in March 1939 with the tragic final defeat of the Republic.

SOLIDARIDAD INTERNACIONAL

So-li-da-ri-dad in-ter-na-cio-nal

o, i, a,

REPUBLICA DEMOCRATICA

RE-PU-BLI-CA DE-MO-CRA-TI-CA

R-e-p-ú-b-l-i-c-a d-e-m-o-c-r-á-t-i-c-a

e, u, i, a, o

R, p, b, l, c, d, m, r, t

LENIN, NUESTRO GRAN MAESTRO

Le-nin, nues-tro gran ma-es-tro

e, i, u, o, a

L, n, s, t, r, g, m

¡VIVA MADRID HEROICO!

VI-VA MA-DRID HE-ROI-CO

Vi-va Ma-drid he-roi-co

i, a, e, o

V, v, M, d, r, h, c

JESUS HERNANDEZ, NUESTRO MINISTRO DE INSTRUCCION

Je-sús Her-nán-dez, nues-tro
Mi-nis-tro de Ins-truc-ción.

J-e-s-ú-s H-e-r-n-á-n-d-e-z, n-u-e-s-t-r-o
M-i-n-i-s-t-r-o d-e I-n-s-t-r-u-c-c-i-ó-n.

i, e, u, a, o
J, s, H, r, n, d, z, M, I.

266

Book cover, *From Beyond: Poems* by Wladyslaw Strzeminski, designed by Julian Przybos, Poland, 1930

Book cover, *Tortilla Flat* by John Steinbeck, designed by Jan Mlodoženiec, Poland, 1957

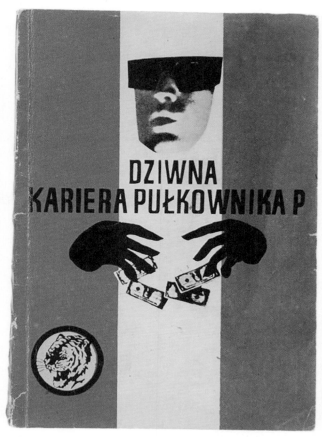

Book cover, *The Strange Case of Colonel P.*, designed by Waldemar Andrzejewski, Poland, 1963

Book cover, *Brain Puzzles*, designed by Janusz Stanny, Poland, c.1960

Book cover, *I Didn't Tell You* by Marian Zatucki, designed by Jerzy Flisak, Poland, 1961

Typeface, Poland, c.1940. Courtesy Jan de Jong Collection

Poster designed by Teresa Zarnower, *Vote for the Unity of Workers and Peasants*, Poland, 1928

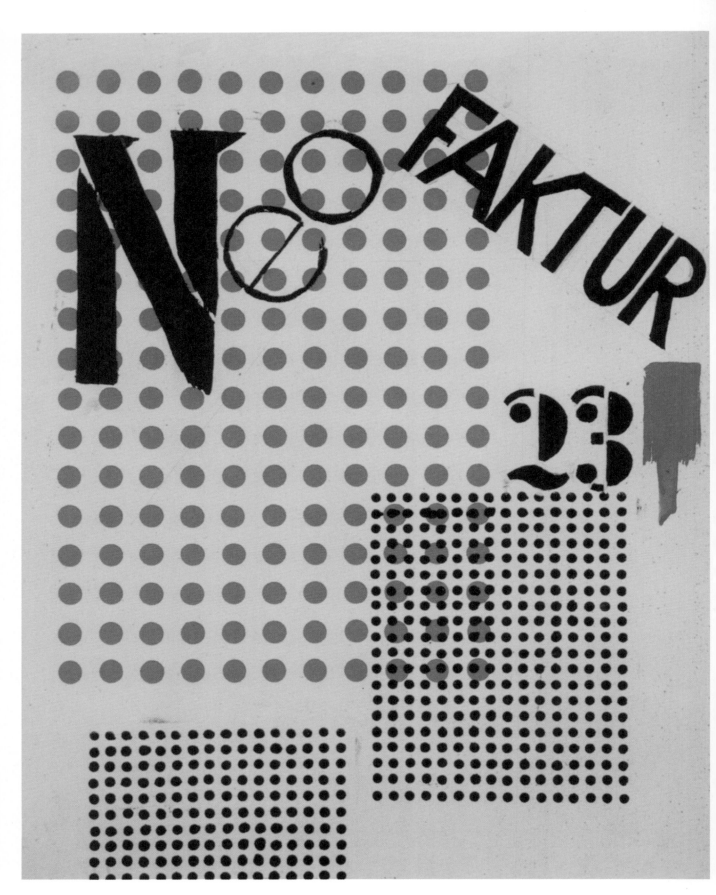

Magazine cover, *Neo-Faktur 23*, designed by Henryk Berlewi, Poland, 1923

274

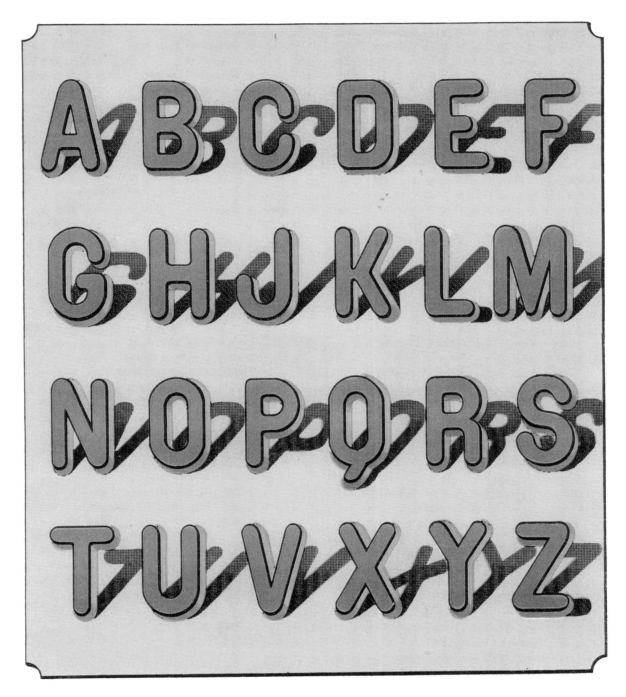

SIGNWRITERS' ALPHABETS

Signwriters' alphabets were designed to be bought off-the-shelf as models for the handpainted lettering of signs and fascia for market stalls, fairground booths, rides, commercial vehicles (trucks, vans, and delivery carts), public transportation vehicles (trains, trams, and buses), and also for printed advertising that aspired to the eye-catching immediacy of such public lettering. They are most often characterized by tromp-l'oeil three-dimensionality, often incorporating an illusionistic shadow, like the shade produced by expensive wooden letter blocks. For well over a century such lettering was an integral visual element of the built environment and a familiar aspect of fairgrounds, seaside piers, and promenades. As times and technologies changed—with the introduction of chrome and neon, for example—such lettering acquired a nostalgic aura and became an evocative sign for times past, worlds lost. Presenting these conventional alphabets as special type specimens creates a reading experience that is elegant, fanciful in color, and original.

From the signwriters' manual *Modèles de Lettres pour peintres en bâtiments*, France, early 1900s. Courtesy Collinge and Clark

From the signwriters' manual *Modèles de Lettres pour peintres en bâtiments*, France, early 1900s. Courtesy Collinge and Clark

From the signwriters' manual *Modèles de Lettres pour peintres en bâtiments*, France, early 1900s. Courtesy Collinge and Clark

From the signwriters' manual *Modèles de Lettres sur des fonds différents*, France, early 1900s. Courtesy Collinge and Clark

From the signwriters' manual *Modèles de Lettres sur des fonds différents*, France, early 1900s. Courtesy Collinge and Clark

From the signwriters' manual *Modèles de Lettres sur des fonds différents*, France, early 1900s. Courtesy Collinge and Clark

From the signwriters' manual *Modèles de Lettres pour peintres en bâtiments*, France, early 1900s. Courtesy Collinge and Clark

From *Album for Signwriters*, the Netherlands, c.1900. Courtesy Jan Tholenaar Collection

From the signwriters' manual *Modèles de Lettres pour peintres en bâtiments*, France, early 1900s. Courtesy Collinge and Clark

Painted sign for a tavern, Russia, c.1910

From *The Sign Writer and Glass Embosser*, UK, 1898. Courtesy Brian Webb collection

From *Album for Signwriters*, the Netherlands, c.1900. Courtesy Jan Tholenaar Collection

From *The Sign Writer and Glass Embosser*, UK, 1898. Courtesy Brian Webb collection

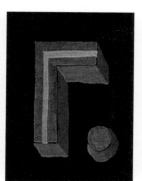

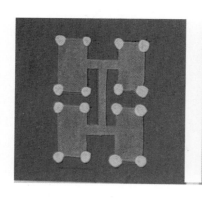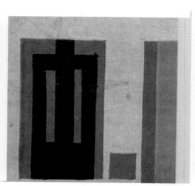

Shop signs and lettering, Greece. Courtesy Alan Fletcher

From the signwriters' manual *Modèles de Lettres pour peintres en bâtiments*, France, early 1900s. Courtesy Collinge and Clark

From the signwriters' manual *Modèles de Lettres sur des fonds differents*, France, early 1900s. Courtesy Collinge and Clark

From the signwriters' manual *Modèles de Lettres sur des fonds differents*, France, early 1900s. Courtesy Collinge and Clark

Painted shop signs, Russia, c.1900

Photo Finsler, 1933: BAG 16 (Wandlampe mit Gleitschuh)

Advertisement for a reading lamp, photograph by Finsler, Germany, 1933. Courtesy Verlag Hermann Schmidt, Mainz

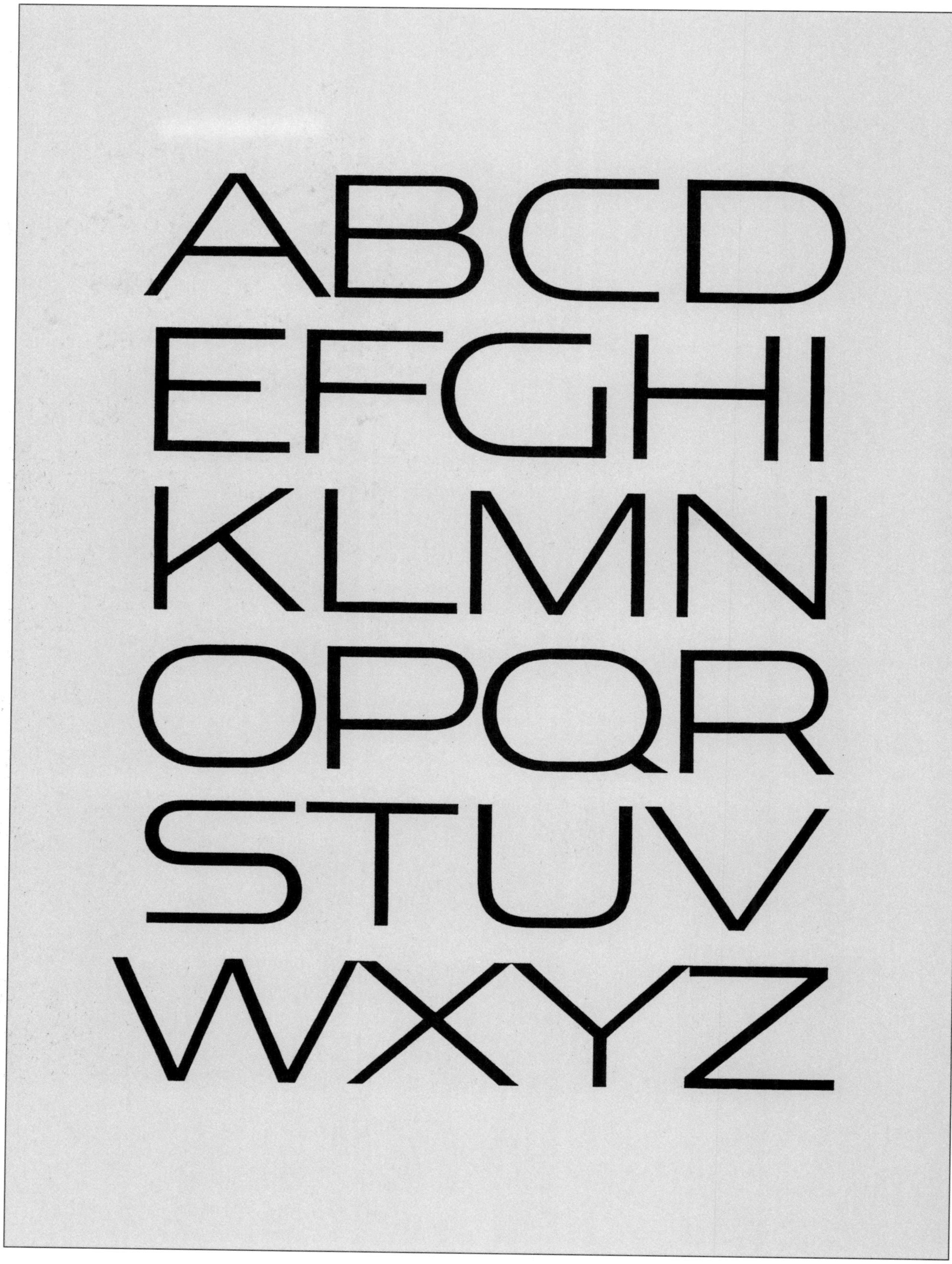

ABCD
EFGHI
KLMN
OPQR
STUV
WXYZ

From the album *Schriften, Lettering, Ecritures*, Germany, 1940s. Courtesy Klingspoor Museum, Offenbach

SOCIETEIT voor CULTUREELE SAMENWERKING

EXCELSIOR THEATER
ZEESTRAAT
GASTVOORSTELLINGEN
DIE JUNGE TRUPPE
(BERLIN)

18 TOT 23 JANUARI 1931
DER ANDERE
VON MIGUEL DE UNAMUNO
DEUTSCH VON OTTO BUCK
DRAMA IN DREI AKTEN MIT EINEM EPILOG

DER ANDERE . . . . GILLIS van RAPPARD

LAURA . . . . ELLEN DAGMAR

DIAMIANA . . . . SYBIL RARES

ERNESTO. . . . . . . EMILIO CARGHER

AVITO . . . . HANS ALVA

DIE AMME. . . . . . . .ERIKA KRISTEN

REGIE: GILLIS van RAPPARD

PRIJZEN DER PLAATSEN
ZAAL 1e DEEL FL. 3.00 ZAAL 2e DEEL FL. 2.50
ZAAL 3e DEEL EN BALCON FL. 1.25
PLAATSEN TE BESPREKEN DAGELIJKS
AAN HET GEBOUW VAN 10 TOT 16 UUR

VAN 24 TOT 31 JANUARI
DIE QUADRATUR DES KREISES
LUSTSPIEL von VAL: KATAJEW

ONTWERP V. HUSZAR

Theater poster designed by Vilmos Huszár, Berlin, 1931

Magazine cover, *Stupid* (No.1, a Dada journal), designed by Franz Wilhelm Seibert, Heinrich and Angelika Hoerle, Germany, 1920

ABCDEFGHIJ
KLMNOPQR
STUVWXYZ

abcdefghi
jklmnopqrsß
tuvwxyz

MOTORRÄDER

From a typefounders' catalogue, Germany, c.1935. Courtesy Verlag Hermann Schmidt, Mainz

Betracht, und so wird auch für die elementare Typographie meist die Groteskschrift verwendet, weil sie das Ursprüngliche in der Schrift am meisten verkörpert und ohne persönliche Merkmale ist. Hier bei dieser Karte aber wurde die Neuland-Type verwendet, ohne störend zu wirken. Mit solchen Experimenten heisst es aber vorsichtig sein. **B** Was soll denn nun aus den vielen anderen schönen Schriften werden, wenn wirklich die neue Kunst um sich greift? **A** Bisher haben die Groteskschriften ungestört in der Ecke gelegen, und nun werden sie eben mal dran kommen. Ist das nicht ein gerechter Ausgleich? **B** Ach, darum ist wohl der Text der Beilage auch gleich so gesetzt, ich meine in Grotesk. Vielleicht gar aus Sympathie? – **A** O, Sie alter Zyniker! Hier kam es doch auf eine ruhige, möglichst kräftige Type an, welche die Beispiele gut hervortreten lässt. **B** Na, klotzig genug sieht sie auch aus. **A** Aber gut in der Flächenwirkung. Wie gefällt Ihnen denn die Aufmachung dieser Beilage in der neuen Art? Jedenfalls ein Mittelweg, der auch für Prospekte usw. gut geeignet wäre. **B** Nun ja, aber ich weiss nicht, hübsch ist anders. **A** Ich finde gerade, dass sich die Seiten mit den Ecken ganz gut ausnehmen. Es liegt Abwechslung darin. **B** Ja, im Fahrten- und Abenteuerbuch liegt auch Abwechslung, ein Bild so und eins so. Ich kann nicht sagen, dass das „sachlich" ist. **A** Freilich hatte auch ich mir gedacht, dass Tschichold andere Wege der Buchkunst finden würde. Vielleicht hat er sich bewusst bezähmt; vielleicht hat auch die Büchergilde ein Wort mitgesprochen. **B** Die werden sowieso am Umsatz der Bücher den „Erfolg" (?) merken! **A** Sie meinen wohl, dass durch die neue Ausstattung die Zahl der Mitglieder steigt? **B** Das wollen wir erst mal sehen! **A** Nun hören Sie mal. Falls Sie auch Lust haben sollten, sich mal in Konstruktivismus zu versuchen, will ich Ihnen ein paar Thesen

mit auf den Weg geben: I. Typographie kann unter Umständen Kunst sein. II. Gestaltung ist Wesen aller Kunst, die typographische Gestaltung ist nicht Abmalen des textlichen Inhalts. III. Auch die nichtbedruckten Stellen sind positive Werte. IV. Qualität der Type bedeutet Einfachheit und Schönheit. Die Einfachheit schliesst in sich Klarheit, eindeutige, zweckentsprechende Form, Verzicht auf allen entbehrlichen Ballast. Schönheit bedeutet gutes Ausbalancieren der Fläche. Die Forderung an die Typographie ist – **B** Hören Sie auf, mir wird ganz schlecht! **A** Schön! Für heute wollen wir dieses Thema abbrechen, beherzigen Sie meine Worte und verwerten Sie das Gute des „Elementaren".

B Eigentlich war es überhaupt Unfug, sich darüber noch lange zu unterhalten und vier Seiten kostbares Papier zu vergeuden, denn wir stehen ja heute mitten im Konstruktivismus, und es wird nicht lange dauern, bis auch diese

BERATUNGEN UND ENTWÜRFE WERBEDRUCKE

GEORG KLEMM NICOLAISTR. 22 FERNRUF 35308

REKLAME DRESDEN–A. 16

GESCHÄFTSKARTE ENTWURF HANS MENKE DRESDEN

Sensation ihr Ende gefunden hat. Denn so war's und ist's noch in der Welt: Im steten Wechsel liegt ja der Reiz des Lebens. **A** Ei, Donnerwetter, Sie sprechen ja so geistreich und verständig! – Gewiss vereinbart sich nicht alles im Konstruktivismus mit unseren bisherigen Anschauungen über Typographie, aber die für ihn erbrachten Begründungen sind nicht ohne weiteres von der Hand zu weisen. Der grösste Teil seiner Widersacher stützt sich meistens auf unbestimmte Gefühle. Wollen wir doch froh sein, dass wir aus der „elementaren typographie" neue Anregungen und Gedanken gewonnen haben, die leider oft in ganz falscher Verkennung der inneren Zusammenhänge weidlich ausgenutzt werden und so bei dem kritischen Beschauer ein nicht immer befriedigendes Gefühl auslösen. **B** Jedenfalls hat man um die neue Art Satzgruppierung, die man plötzlich mit „Kunst" bezeichnet, viel zuviel Wesens gemacht. Drum sei auch der Debatte ein Punkt gesetzt.

From *Typographic News*, Germany, c.1926. Courtesy Verlag Hermann Schmidt, Mainz

Magazine cover, *Gebrauchsgraphik*, Germany, 1930s. Courtesy Gutenberg Museum, Mainz

Back cover, *Gebrauchsgraphik*, Germany, 1926. Courtesy Gutenberg Museum, Mainz

ABCDEEF
GHIJKLM
NOPQRS
TU8VWX
YZ
ĥĩĭĩ[ĩĮĻ

DIE
CENCI

WORTH
7. RUE DE LA PAIX

DEUTSCHE
OPAK
GLAS
WERKE

RUSCHEWEYH
MÖBEL

RUSCHEWEYH
TISCHE

abcdefghijklmno
pqrfstuvwxyz
ABCDEFGHIJKLMN
OPQRSTUVWXYZ

KONSTRUIERTE SCHRIFTEN

From *Hoffmann's Schriftatlas*, Germany, 1930

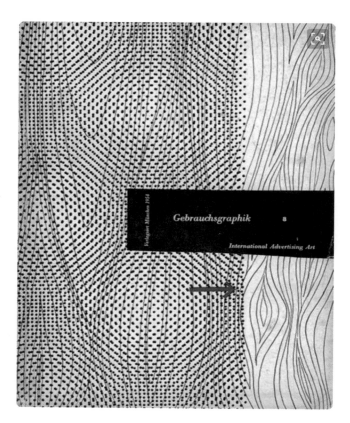

Magazine covers, *Gebrauchsgraphik,* Germany, LEFT: 1954 RIGHT: 1930

Magazine covers, *Gebrauchsgraphik*, Germany, LEFT: 1925 RIGHT: 1954

Magazine cover, *Gebrauchsgraphik*, Germany, 1924. Courtesy Gutenberg Museum, Mainz

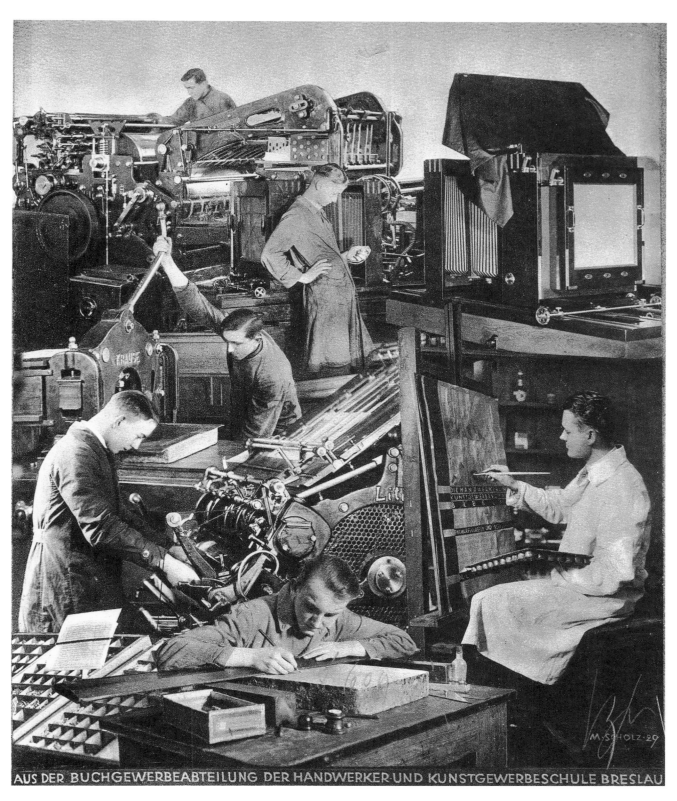

AUS DER BUCHGEWERBEABTEILUNG DER HANDWERKER UND KUNSTGEWERBESCHULE BRESLAU

Photomontage by M. Scholz from *Gebrauchsgraphik*, Germany, 1929

TOP: Leaflet designed by Herbert Bayer, Germany, 1928 BOTTOM: Advertisement for a printer from *Gebrauchsgraphik*, Germany, 1930

ELEMENTARE
TYPOGRAPHIE
MIT
ERBAR
GROTESK
SCHRIFTEN
DER
SCHRIFTGIESSEREI
LUDWIG
&MAYER
FRANKFURT
AM MAIN

BEILAGE ZUR „GEBRAUCHSGRAPHIK"
ENTWURF, SATZ UND DRUCK
KÖLNER WERKSCHULEN
KLASSE ERBAR

Leaflet promoting the typeface *Erbar*, Germany, 1930

Preliminary drawing for the typeface *Futura*, Paul Renner, Germany, 1925

Publicity announcement in *Gebrauchsgraphik*, Germany, 1930

Collage by Robert Michel, Germany, 1927

THE END